*authentically,*

*uniquely*

*you*

LIVING FREE FROM COMPARISON
AND THE NEED TO PLEASE

authentically,
uniquely
you

JOYCE MEYER

HODDER &
STOUGHTON

First published in Great Britain in 2021 by Hodder & Stoughton
An Hachette UK company

Published in association with FaithWords
A division of Hachette Book Group, Inc.

2

A CIP catalogue record for this title is available from the British Library

Trade Paperback ISBN 978 1 529 37525 1
eBook ISBN 978 1 529 37527 5

Printed and bound in Great Britain by Clays Ltd, Elcograf S.p.A.

Hodder & Stoughton policy is to use papers that are natural, renewable and recyclable products and made from wood grown in sustainable forests. The logging and manufacturing processes are expected to conform to the environmental regulations of the country of origin.

Hodder & Stoughton Ltd
Carmelite House
50 Victoria Embankment
London EC4Y 0DZ

www.hodderfaith.com

# CONTENTS

Being our authentic and unique selves in a world that seeks to conform us to its image or tries to make us something we are not is a challenge we will deal with most of our lives. We are all unique, and that is good. The qualities that make us special benefit us and bless others in many ways. According to God's design, no one person is precisely like anyone else. Even identical twins have different fingerprints and different iris patterns in their eyes. Their DNA is very similar, but not *exactly* the same.

There is no one else in the world exactly like you. This not only makes you unique; it also makes you very special. One-of-a-kind things are usually very valuable and highly sought after. This makes me wonder why so many of us try to be like other people. Many of us put great effort into trying to be—or appearing to be—someone or something we are not. I believe we do this because we have not accepted and embraced ourselves, and we fear that other people will not accept us either.

I suffered for many years trying to be like people I admired—at least I admired the traits I saw in them that I did not see in myself. I had not yet learned that God gives each of us unique traits, but He does not give us all *the same* unique traits. We are all good at some things, but no one is good at everything. Accepting this is the first step toward being at peace with ourselves and with other people.

It is possible to try so hard to be like so many other people that we forget who we are. During his acting career, Peter Sellers played so many roles that he sometimes lost himself in the characters he played. When approached by a fan who asked, "Are you Peter Sellers?" he answered briskly, "Not today," and walked on.

When we allow other people to pressure us to be someone we are not, we can become frustrated. The people around us can become equally frustrated when we expect them to do things they are not gifted to do or to be anyone other than themselves. Jesus came to set us free, and part of the freedom He offers is the liberty to be and enjoy who we are without comparing ourselves to or competing with others.

People who are authentic have accepted their uniqueness and have learned to enjoy themselves as they are. They do not struggle to be what other people want them to be but desire to be who God has created them to be and to have the courage to follow their own heart as He leads them. They have no need to pretend or be hypocritical. Instead, they have pure hearts and right motives for all they do. They like who they are, and they enjoy being at peace with themselves.

We all have room for improvement in our character and in our behavior, and we can and should work with the Holy Spirit to make the changes that are needed in our lives. But we also have many qualities that, although we may not like them, we cannot change because God has made them part of who we are. For example, I spent years not liking my voice because it is deeper than most female voices, and I am often mistaken for a man when I call people who don't know me. However, eventually I realized that God gave me my unique voice for His purpose, and I learned to accept and enjoy it.

We might be tempted to worry about the aspects of ourselves we would like to change, but Jesus says that worry cannot add a single hour to our lives (Matthew 6:27). God has already thought through the shape of our lives, and no amount of work or struggle can ever change them.

More than forty years of experience in ministry has taught me that unhappy, frustrated people are usually that way because they don't like themselves. Instead of accepting themselves and becoming all that God wants them to be, they continually strive to be what others want them to be or what they imagine they should be. We all want to please people, and God's Word tells us that we should strive to live in harmony with others, even when it comes at a cost (Romans 12:16 and 15:1). However, if pleasing people causes us not to please God, then we must obey God, not other people (Acts 5:29).

One of the best gifts you can give yourself is to accept yourself and believe that God created you with His own hand in your mother's womb. All of His works are wonderful—and that includes you (Psalm 139:13–16). I pray that, as you read this book, you will learn to embrace your unique self and live authentically and that you will find freedom from comparing yourself to others and from trying to please people in unhealthy ways. I also pray that, in your life, you will set boundaries that keep you safe from letting others control or manipulate you and that you will find the freedom to be the amazing person God intends for you to be.

# PART 1

# Believing the Best about Yourself

# CHAPTER 1

# Learning to Love Who You Are

*Love your neighbor as yourself.*

Matthew 22:39

Learning to accept and love ourselves is the pathway to authenticity, because if we reject ourselves and refuse God's love for us, we will not be free to be ourselves. Instead, we will live a life of pretense, choosing to do what we think will make us acceptable to others rather than what we honestly believe we should do. Even though our hearts scream no in certain situations, we will find our mouths saying yes to the things people want us to do.

Let me ask you: Do you love yourself? To love yourself is to accept the unconditional love of God with your whole heart, to see yourself as He sees you, and to rejoice and be at peace with who He has created you to be. I am not talking about loving yourself in a selfish or self-centered way, but loving the unique *you* that God created you to be. This healthy self-love is not based on what you do right or wrong, but on who you are in Christ. Truly believing that God loves you unconditionally is the foundation for relationship with Him, with yourself, and with others.

No one will love everything they do, but we should all love who God has made us to be. Depending on the translation, the Bible says at least eight times that we should love our neighbor as we love ourselves. It is so significant to God that we love ourselves that He based another of His most important instructions to us—to love others—on this foundation. And He didn't say it just once, but multiple times.

Why is it so important that we love ourselves? First, if we don't love ourselves, we reject God's love for us. Second, if we don't love ourselves, we cannot love God or anyone else. The Holy Spirit fills us with God's love, and He wants us to let that love flow through us back to God and out to others. God's Word says that we love Him because He first loved us (1 John 4:19). If we have not received God's love, we have no love to give to anyone else, because no matter how much we want to love people, we cannot give away what we do not have. I spent many frustrating years as a Christian trying to love others and failing until the Lord showed me that my problem was that I had never truly received His love for me.

After receiving this revelation, I spent one year studying, meditating on, and confessing aloud God's love for me. At that time, I had a forty-year history of not liking myself, let alone loving myself, so renewing my mind in this area took time. At first, I felt guilty trying to love myself because I was keenly aware of my flaws, but eventually I learned that I could love who I am without loving everything I do. We can all work with God toward positive change in our behavior without rejecting ourselves or viewing ourselves as a failure because of our imperfections.

> I learned that I could love who I am without loving everything I do.

For many years, I tended to do what I thought would please other people instead of what I genuinely thought I should do or wanted to do. Since I didn't love myself, I desperately tried to get the love I was missing from people by allowing them to control and manipulate me. I thought that as long as I did everything they wanted me to do, I would have their love and acceptance, but I soon found that the minute I didn't please them, they rejected me. This experience helped me understand the importance of receiving God's love for me and loving myself in a healthy, biblical way.

Being able to love yourself is the key to much joy, peace, and confidence in life. Right here, before you read any further, I encourage

> Being able to love yourself is the key to much joy, peace, and confidence in life.

you to ask God to use this book to help you love yourself more than ever. It will make a wonderful difference in your life.

## Self-Acceptance Leads to Power

God wants us to have confidence in His unconditional love for us. We are mistaken if we think that disliking or hating ourselves is an expression of humility, because it is not. The apostle John had a deep revelation of how much God loved him. He repeatedly referred to himself as "the disciple whom Jesus loved" (John 13:23; 21:7, 20). This may come across as prideful, but it actually reflects the way God wants us to think of ourselves. Knowing and abiding in God's love makes us powerful.

Knowing and living in the love of God makes us powerful because it sets us free from self-doubt and enables us to trust God to do great things in us and through us. It also liberates us from caring too much about what other people think about us and allows us to seek to please God alone, instead of trying to please other people. It makes us feel strong and able to follow our hearts, express ourselves, and live the lives God intends for us. It helps us focus on what is right and good about us, not what is wrong with us. When we live with the awareness that God loves us, and when we love ourselves, there's no limit to what God can do through us or to the enjoyment we can find in our lives.

## Be at Peace with Yourself

First Peter 3:11 is one of my favorite scriptures: "Let him search for peace…and seek it eagerly. [Do not merely desire peaceful relations with God, with your fellowmen, and with yourself, but pursue, go after them!]" (AMPC).

*Pursue* is a strong word. It requires action. To pursue peace is to do whatever it takes to maintain peace in our lives. It means not always getting our way or having the last word in an argument. It requires us to trust God with the people in our lives instead of trying to force them to be what we want them to be. But it's all worth it because it brings peace, and peace is one of the most valuable qualities we can have.

Here are some ways you can cultivate peace with God, yourself, and others:

### 1. Receive God's forgiveness.

Peace with God is the foundation for peace in every other area of our lives. Jesus is the "Prince of Peace" (Isaiah 9:6), and only through a relationship with Him will we ever experience true contentment.

When we sin, the best way to respond is to repent, ask God to forgive us, and then choose not to allow feelings of guilt to torment us. Guilt is useless. Constantly feeling guilty actually weakens us and causes us to fall into more sin.

I encourage you to read and meditate on 1 John 1:9: "If we

[freely] admit that we have sinned and confess our sins, He is faithful and just . . . and will forgive our sins [dismiss our lawlessness] and [continuously] cleanse us from all unrighteousness" (AMPC).

## 2. Make the decision to like yourself.

This question may seem unusual, but what kind of relationship do you have with yourself? You can't get along with anyone else until you get along with you. Eleanor Roosevelt rightly observed, "Before we can make friends with anyone else, we must first make friends with ourselves."

> What kind of relationship do you have with yourself?

For years, I dealt with self-hatred because of the sexual abuse I endured growing up. Because I didn't like myself, enjoying peace with anyone was almost impossible for me. However, as I spent time in God's Word and asked Him to change me, I eventually began to see myself the way He sees me. I began to like myself, and eventually love myself!

I encourage you to find out what God says about you in His Word. Ask Him to help you change your self-image, because enjoying life and enjoying other people begins with knowing who God says you are and loving yourself in a balanced way.

## 3. Don't compare yourself to others.

Comparing and competing with other people puts you on a fast track to losing your peace and joy. There is such freedom in learning to be happy with who you are without being jealous of someone else's skills or achievements.

I have a friend who likes to memorize parts of the Bible. There was a day when I would have been threatened by that, feeling that I should do it too. I know a lot of Scripture, and I have even memorized several verses, but memorization has never been my strength, and that's okay. It doesn't mean I am less spiritual or somehow not as good as my friend. It just means I am being myself.

## 4. Accept other people just the way they are, not the way you want them to be.

I almost wore myself out trying to change people until I realized everyone is not supposed to be like I am. We are all born with different God-given temperaments, and we were never meant to be the same.

My husband, Dave, is easygoing and has the ability to enjoy just about anything he does. I'll never forget our grocery trips as a young married couple. I had my list and was serious about accomplishing our mission. Dave, on the other hand, was pushing the kids around in the cart, laughing, and having a great time. That behavior infuriated me! Usually, when people are miserable, they resent those who are joyful.

Dave has always been a very wise and responsible man, but I wanted him to be "serious," like I am. When I finally stopped trying to change him, it brought tremendous peace. Now, I truly enjoy and value Dave's personality. In fact, through the years the Lord has helped me to enjoy my life and be more like Dave is, even though I have not consciously tried to do so.

We all have areas in which we truly need to change, but only God can change us. The best gift we can give to others is to pray for them and accept them as they are. We may need to confront certain bad behaviors in them, but if we constantly find fault with others, then we need to look at our own attitude instead of their behavior.

## 5. *Let God have control of your life.*

Proverbs 16:9 says, "A man's mind plans his way, but the Lord directs his steps and makes them sure" (AMPC). I used to have a plan for everything—including my husband, my children, and my ministry—and sometimes grew frustrated if every aspect of it didn't go accordingly. In other words, I wanted the Lord to do things my way! However, God is smarter than we are, and He wants us to place our trust in His great plan for our lives.

I often say that trust requires unanswered questions. In the moment, we may not always understand why, but as David says to God in Psalm 31:15, "My times are in your hands." Even though we may not understand something that is taking place in our lives, we will later look back and discover that the Lord had our best interests in mind all along.

I encourage you to continue trusting God even when things don't make sense. It's one sure way to enjoy your life and experience more peace than ever before.

## Self-Rejection Leads to People-Pleasing

When we reject ourselves, we assume other people will reject us too. When we struggle with self-rejection, we don't wait to find out how they will treat us, but we proactively think and believe they will reject us. This causes us to behave in ways that will guarantee their rejection, which confirms our belief that we are not likable or lovable. If we fear that people will reject us, we lose our authenticity by trying to please them in order to gain their acceptance. This sets up a cycle that continues until we break it.

There are people in the world who like to control and prey on people who are insecure and are easily manipulated. They take advantage of the fact that these people are starving for friendship, love, and companionship. But people who are confident and love themselves as God loves them won't put up with those who seek to control others for their own self-gratification. People who have a healthy self-confidence and self-love will confront these unhealthy people and set boundaries that must be honored if their relationship is to grow.

My father was a controller, and because of our fear of him, everyone in our family allowed him to take the lead in everything from what we watched on television, to what time we went to bed and got up, to who our friends could be (if we were allowed to have any), to what meals consisted of—down to the tiniest details of our lives. When people are allowed no freedom of choice, their souls are damaged in ways that often require years to heal.

Because my father was never satisfied with me, no matter what I did, I learned to never be satisfied with myself. Therefore, I certainly could not believe that God, my heavenly Father, was pleased with me as Scripture says that He is. If you grew up with controlling parents, you know what I am talking about. Let me encourage you; instead of basing your beliefs about yourself on what others have told you or how they have behaved toward you, find out what God says about you in His Word and believe it.

For example, He says:

- You are the apple of His eye (Zechariah 2:8).
- You are chosen by Him (1 Corinthians 1:27; John 15:16).
- He will never reject you when you come to Him (John 6:37).
- His love is everlasting (Jeremiah 31:3).
- You are special, a chosen people, a royal priesthood, God's special possession (1 Peter 2:9).
- You have gifts, skills, and talents (1 Peter 4:10).
- You are made right with Him through Jesus Christ (2 Corinthians 5:21).

The Lord makes many other wonderful statements about you in His Word, and believing them will change your life.

If God—who is perfect—loves and accepts you, there is no reason for you not to do likewise. We usually determine whether or not we are lovable based on how we feel, but our feelings are always changing. Therefore, we cannot trust them to represent the truth. God and His Word are truth, and it is impossible for Him to lie (John 14:6; Hebrews 6:18). We can depend on Him completely.

## Ask Yourself

We all need to face our struggles in order to be set free. I'd like to ask you a few questions to help you face any issues that may be holding you back.

- Do you believe that God loves you?
- Do you love and accept yourself?
- Are you a people-pleaser?
- Are you at peace with yourself?

- Do you fear rejection?
- Do you compare yourself with others?

Simply taking a few moments to ponder these questions before you keep reading will help you identify areas of your life in which you may need help.

CHAPTER 2

# Your Self-Image Matters

*The worst loneliness is not to be comfortable with yourself.*

Mark Twain

Your self-image, meaning how you see and think about yourself, is very important, so I believe it is worth taking some time to consider. What others think of you isn't nearly as important as what you think of yourself. God's Word teaches us not to think more highly of ourselves than we ought to (2 Corinthians 3:5), but neither should we think of ourselves as

> What others think of you isn't nearly as important as what you think of yourself.

being less than we are in Christ. No matter what we are capable of, we won't do it if we don't *believe* we are capable of doing it.

We are not to think as the world does, but we should learn to think as God does, according to His Word. The world teaches us to think that:

- Our acceptance is based on our performance.
- We will be rejected if we do not please people.
- We are loved only if we merit being loved.
- Nothing is free.
- We must compete with others to be first.

- We are more valuable if we look right, do right, know the right people, live in the right neighborhood, are talented, and have the right job.

Jesus says that:

- He accepts us unconditionally based on faith alone.
- He never rejects us as long as we believe in Him.
- He loves us unconditionally.
- God's love is a gift. Our salvation and everything else we receive from God comes not by our works, but by His grace (goodness).
- We are to love other people, not compete with them.
- We believe His promises, and He provides.

The world says we should strive to get to the top, but God says the first will be last and the last will be first (Matthew 20:16). True promotion comes from Him. Our value is in nothing we can do, but in Christ.

## In Christ

Because I refer frequently to being "in Christ," I want to make sure you understand what this term means. When we receive Jesus as our Savior, He comes to live in our spirit (the inmost part of us) and our life is in Him. We abide (live, dwell, remain) in Him (John 15:5, 7). We live in Him by faith, by believing what His Word says. Because God sees us "in Christ," every victory Jesus has won becomes our victory also. When He died, we died, and when He was raised, we too were raised (Romans 6:4–5). He is seated in the heavenly realms (Ephesians 1:20), and we are seated in Him (Ephesians 2:6).

The Bible makes at least seven important points about who we are in Christ, and they will help you understand how powerful our position in Him is.

## 1. In Christ, you are saved and called to a holy life.

He has saved us and called us to a holy life—not because of anything we have done but because of his own purpose and grace. This grace was given us in Christ Jesus before the beginning of time.

2 Timothy 1:9

## 2. In Christ, God sees you as holy and blameless.

For he chose us in him before the creation of the world to be holy and blameless in his sight.

Ephesians 1:4

## 3. In Christ, you are sealed (protected and preserved) by the Holy Spirit.

And you also were included in Christ when you heard the message of truth, the gospel of your salvation. When you believed, you were marked in him with a seal, the promised Holy Spirit.

Ephesians 1:13

## 4. In Christ, you can never be separated from God's love.

For I am convinced that neither death nor life, neither angels nor demons, neither the present nor the future, nor any powers, neither height nor depth, nor anything else in all creation, will be able to separate us from the love of God that is in Christ Jesus our Lord.

Romans 8:38–39

### 5. In Christ, you are fully forgiven and redeemed.

In him we have redemption through his blood, the forgiveness of sins, in accordance with the riches of God's grace.

Ephesians 1:7

### 6. In Christ, you are justified before God and righteous in His sight.

God made him who had no sin to be sin for us, so that in him we might become the righteousness of God.

2 Corinthians 5:21

### 7. In Christ, your old life has passed away. You have been made new.

Therefore, if anyone is in Christ, the new creation has come: The old has gone, the new is here!

2 Corinthians 5:17

Once you believe in Christ, trust Him as your Savior, and understand the difference between who you are in Christ and who you are in yourself, you no longer struggle to try to earn or deserve what is already yours as a gift from God.

In addition to the list above, consider also these realities about who you are in Christ:

- Your value is in Christ (Psalm 139:13–16; 1 Peter 1:18–19).
- Your confidence is in Christ (Philippians 3:3).
- You can do all things through Christ who is your strength (Philippians 4:13).
- You are complete in Christ (Colossians 2:10).
- You have the mind of Christ (1 Corinthians 2:16).
- You are God's handiwork, created in Christ to do good works (Ephesians 2:10).
- You are a co-heir with Christ (Romans 8:17).
- You are more than a conqueror through Christ (Romans 8:37).

Each time you see the phrase "in Christ" in your Bible or in this book, pay close attention to it, because it tells you of something that belongs to you because of God's grace, something that you do not have to strive for but that you receive through faith. In Christ, your old nature has died. You are now a new creation, and God's nature lives in you through the power of the Holy Spirit.

You may ask, "If all of this is true, then why do I still behave in ways that are ungodly?" The answer is simple: You are in the process of growing into the person you already are in Christ. God sees you complete and finished. He sees you from His perspective, not from an earthly perspective. The Holy Spirit is working with you and in you, transforming you into the image of Jesus (Romans 8:29).

Think of it this way: A mother is out shopping and finds a fantastic sale on clothes for boys' size 4–6. Her son is still too small for that size, but she buys them anyway, knowing that he will grow into them. God knows that we will grow into all He has provided for us as we continue in His Word and walk in His will.

## What Do You Think of Yourself?

Having a healthy, godly view of yourself is extremely important. Among other things, it will determine your level of confidence, affect the way you evaluate the opportunities that come your way, and influence your relationships with God and others. Consider this, for example: You can be wonderfully talented, but if you think you are not, you will not manifest (display or exercise) the talent you have. The same is true for any other ability or characteristic. Below is a list of thoughts that I believe reflect an acceptable, godly, and balanced attitude to have toward yourself:

- I know God created me, and He loves me (Psalm 139:13–18; John 15:9).
- I have faults and weaknesses, and I want to change. I believe God is working in my life. He is changing me little by little, day by day. While He is doing so, I can still enjoy my life and myself (2 Corinthians 3:18).
- I celebrate the progress I have made instead of being discouraged about how far I still have to go (Philippians 1:6).
- Everyone has faults. I am not a failure simply because I am not yet perfect in my behavior (Philippians 3:12–14).
- I am working with God to overcome my weaknesses, but I realize that I will always be growing in some area. I will not become discouraged when God convicts me of areas in my life that need improvement (Hebrews 12:5–12).
- I want to make people happy and have them like me, but my sense of worth is not dependent on what others think of me.

Jesus has already affirmed my value by His willingness to die for me (John 15:13).

- I will not allow what people think, say, or do to control me. Even if they totally reject me, I will survive, because God has promised to never reject or condemn me as long as I believe in Him (Hebrews 13:6).

- No matter how often I fail, I will not give up, because Jesus is with me to strengthen and sustain me. He has promised to never leave me or forsake me (Hebrews 13:5).

- I like myself. I don't like everything I do, and I want to change, but I refuse to reject myself (Romans 8:1).

- I am right with God through Jesus Christ (2 Corinthians 5:21).

- God has a good plan for my life. I will fulfill my destiny and be all I can be for His glory. I have God-given talents and abilities, and I intend to use them to help others (Jeremiah 29:11; Ephesians 2:10; Hebrews 13:20–21).

- I am nothing in myself, and yet, in Christ, I am everything I need to be (John 15:4–5).

- I can do everything I need to do—everything that God calls me to do—through His Son, Jesus Christ (Philippians 4:13).

## What Happens When You Think Too Little of Yourself?

God's Word gives us at least two great examples of what happens when we belittle ourselves in our own thinking. In Numbers 13:17–33, Moses sent twelve spies to spy out the Promised Land to see if it was indeed as good as God had said it would be. The fruit in that land was huge and, I'm sure, delicious. Carrying just a single cluster of grapes on a pole required two men. That land was wonderful, but giants called the Nephilim were there. Because of them, ten of the twelve spies allowed fear to defeat them and began to think of themselves as grasshoppers (Numbers 13:33). Because of the weak, negative way they viewed themselves, their enemies viewed them as weak as well.

The two remaining spies, Joshua and Caleb, saw the giants, but they also saw God and believed He was well able to defeat the Nephilim. Sadly, the ten fearful men saw the giants and looked at their own ability instead of looking to God. Their grasshopper image kept them from enjoying the life God had ordained for them. These men believed in God and had been taught all their lives about His power and goodness, but when their faith was tested, they failed to believe in what God could do through them if they would trust Him.

> Don't make the mistake of looking at your own weaknesses. Look at Jesus and His ability instead.

Don't make the mistake of looking at your own weaknesses. Look at Jesus and His ability instead. What is impossible with man is possible with God. All things are possible with Him (Mark 10:27).

A second example of how powerful our thoughts toward ourselves can be is in 2 Samuel 9:1–13. King Saul and his son, Jonathan, were both deceased, and David was now king. Because he had been in a covenant relationship with Jonathan, he was searching for any of Jonathan's relatives so he could bless them for Jonathan's sake. He heard about a young man named Mephibosheth, who was living an impoverished life in a town called Lo Debar. Because this young man was Saul's grandson and Jonathan's son, he was entitled to be provided for with excellence. When David located him, the boy fell down in front of him in fear and offered to be David's servant. David told him not to fear, because he intended to show him kindness for the sake of Jonathan, his father. David told Mephibosheth that he would restore all of Saul's land to him and that he would always eat at the king's table.

The boy's response reveals why he was living such an impoverished life, when in reality he was entitled to untold riches and honor. Mephibosheth answered, "What is your servant, that you should notice a dead dog like me?" (2 Samuel 9:8). He had a very low opinion of himself. Perhaps this was because he was made lame as a child when the nurse carrying him fell while trying to escape the palace after they heard that Saul and Jonathan had died in battle, and David was to be king (2 Samuel 4:4). They had no real reason to be afraid of David, but rumors had filled them with fear and poisoned their thinking. David reminded the boy of who he was and helped him change his attitude toward himself. Mephibosheth finished his life in proper style, eating always at the king's table.

Sometimes we are like Mephibosheth. We see the areas of our lives in which we are crippled or handicapped (areas of weakness), and we begin to think they disqualify us from the privileges God has promised us. However, we must realize that our weaknesses do not annul God's strength. The Lord told Paul that His strength was made perfect in weakness and that He would give him enough grace to enable him to do whatever He had called Paul to do (2 Corinthians 12:9–10).

The ten spies who saw themselves as grasshoppers and Mephibosheth, who saw himself as a dead dog, all had a poor self-image that kept them from being, doing, and having all that God had planned for them. If you have developed a poor self-image because of things that have been done to you or said to you, don't let it hold you back now that Jesus is in your life. Remember, you are a "new creation" and "the old has gone, the new is here!" (2 Corinthians 5:17).

You are a new creation, and you have a new life in Christ, because that's what God's Word says. But you may still struggle with old thoughts, especially thoughts about yourself. The way you view yourself matters, and it affects everything about your life, so developing a healthy, godly self-image is extremely important.

In the back of this book, you will find an appendix titled "Fifty Scriptures that Affirm God's Love for You." If you want your self-image to reflect what God thinks about you and how He feels toward you, let me encourage you to read, study, meditate on, memorize, and speak these scriptures aloud as often as possible. The more you think about what God's Word says about you, the more you will believe it and live from it.

# CHAPTER 3

# Authenticity

*These people honor me with their lips, but their hearts are far from me.*

Matthew 15:8

To be authentic means to be genuine and real, not to be a pretender. Authentic people have a pure heart. They don't pretend to be something they are not. They don't behave one way with some people and another way with other people simply to fit in, impress, or be accepted.

> To be authentic means to be genuine and real, not to be a pretender.

Jesus had scathing words for the religious pretenders of His day. He called them "whitewashed tombs, which look beautiful on the outside but on the inside are full of the bones of the dead and everything unclean" (Matthew 23:27). Most of Matthew 23 is a rebuke of the religious Pharisees, who were not authentic and genuine. They had impure motives, and Jesus said they were hypocrites, telling others what to do but not doing it themselves (vv. 3–4). He told them that they did everything hoping that people would see them (v. 5). They loved to sit in places of honor so they would appear to be important (v. 6). Having people think well of them meant more to them than having a pure and sincere heart. Jesus said they were careful to follow all the laws, but neglected

mercy, justice, and faithfulness—qualities that were more important than keeping all the rules (v. 23).

In essence, they were fakes and phonies, pretenders who cared
more about their reputation with people than they did about their
reputation with God. They were not authentic. They were people-
pleasers, not God-pleasers.

## Fake Worship

People who are not genuine in their worship of God go through
the motions of worship repetitiously without giving any thought
to their meaning (Isaiah 29:13). It is easy to mouth words from a
hymnal or a giant screen at the front of a sanctuary yet be thinking about something entirely different. I can remember singing
songs in church while thinking about taking revenge against my
husband because I was angry with him about something he'd
done before we arrived at church that morning. I could sing the
old hymn "I Surrender All" while thinking, *If he thinks I am going
to cook him a big meal today, he is wrong!* Such an attitude sounds
terrible now, even as I write it, but at the time I was not aware of
how important authenticity was. We are to love God with all of
our heart, soul, and mind (Matthew 22:37). We should love and
worship Him with our whole heart, not with a divided heart or
with our mind on something else.

Think about how easy it is to sing songs of worship while
inwardly judging how the person in front of us looks or thinking about what we dislike about someone singing in the choir
or on the worship team. People cannot see our hearts, but God
does, and He is more concerned with our having a pure heart
than hearing us sing a thousand songs that have no real meaning
to us.

It is not enough to sing songs of worship in a church service and then dishonor God with our behavior when we are at home, at work, or in a social setting. Jesus said that a time would come when people would genuinely and sincerely worship God "in the Spirit and in truth" (John 4:23–24). This is the only kind of worship that is acceptable to Him. We should worship God with our lives, not just our lips.

> *We should worship God with our lives, not just our lips.*

The Old Testament prophet Elijah challenged the people around him, asking them how long they would "waver between two opinions" (1 Kings 18:21). They were trying to serve the Lord God and the false god Baal at the same time, and Elijah knew that would never work. Sometimes we try to be God-pleasers and people-pleasers at the same time, and we too will eventually have to embrace one and let the other go, because God is a jealous God (Exodus 34:14). He will never be satisfied with anything less than whole-hearted devotion.

## Love Not the World

Scripture says quite a bit about trying to serve God with a divided heart. We can't serve two masters wholeheartedly (Matthew 6:24). The apostle John writes that if we love the world and the things in it, we cannot also love the Father (1 John 2:15). There are many Christians—and I was one previously—who are not fully committed to the Lord. I often say they want enough of Jesus to stay out of hell, but not enough to truly live for Him and keep Him first in their lives. I think we all reach a point of decision where we must decide whether or not we will serve God authentically, with all of our heart, and refuse to compromise, even if it means the loss of relationships and having those we hoped would accept us actually judge and criticize us.

We can and should enjoy things that are beautiful, clean, pure, good, and wholesome. God wants us to laugh often and enjoy the life He has provided for us, but we must not love and be attached to the *things* that are in the world or compromise our godly values in order to have them. This becomes a test for every Christian at some time, but we can pass that test and keep God as our number-one priority. Remember that Jesus says to seek first God's kingdom and His righteousness, and everything else will be added to us (Matthew 6:33). We don't have to seek things or compromise our morals in order to get them. We can seek God and be assured that He will provide us with all that we need.

## Let Your Love Be Sincere

We can never be authentic unless we take an honest look at the motives behind what we do. Pure motives are very important to the Lord and should be very important to us, too. They are also crucial to having good relationships with people. The Word of God teaches us that our love should be *sincere* (Romans 12:9), which is another word for *authentic*.

Why would we pretend to love or like someone if we are not sincere about it? We do it because we want something from that person. I can recall times in my life when I paid a great deal of attention to someone or gave them insincere compliments because I wanted something from them or wanted them to think well of me. Have you ever done that?

When we behave this way, it may be because the people with whom we are being phony can promote us on the job, and even though we don't like them, we pretend to, hoping for advancement. Or we may do it because being connected with certain people gives us a better status with others at work, in the neighborhood, or at school. We might even give them gifts or do other favors for them, but we are doing those deeds so they will think well of us or so that others will admire us for our good works. God's Word teaches us not to do our good deeds so that people will witness them or for recognition or earthly praise (Matthew 6:1–6). I try to practice not telling

> *It is amazing how difficult it is to do good things for people and not tell anyone.*

anyone what I have done for others in accordance with the scripture. It is amazing how difficult it is to do good things for people and not tell anyone, but we can be satisfied knowing that God sees all we do, and our reward will come from Him.

> But when you give to the needy, do not let your left hand know what your right hand is doing, so that your giving may be in secret. Then your Father, who sees what is done in secret, will reward you.
>
> Matthew 6:3–4

However, just last week I gave three different people some money to help them during a time when a lot of people had lost their jobs, and I did tell someone about those gifts. When I realized what I had done, I asked myself why I talked about those situations, and I realized I was hoping to motivate the person I told about them to be more generous. Was my motive good or bad? I should have prayed for that person instead of bragging on myself, hoping to motivate him. There must have been a little something in me that wanted him to think I was "good" because of my giving. I repented as soon as I realized what I had done, but I share this story so you will realize how easy it is to brag on ourselves and then think we are doing it for noble reasons. Getting deeply honest with ourselves can be painful, but it is only the truth that makes us free (John 8:32).

There are times when we do our good deeds in front of people so they will glorify God (Matthew 5:16), but those times should definitely be Spirit led. What matters most is having pure motives.

Our motives are very important to God. He isn't as interested in *what* we do as He is in *why* we do it. I will cover this subject in more detail later in the book, but for now I simply encourage you to start asking yourself why you are doing the things you do in order to help you understand whether they are authentic and pleasing to God or not.

## Sincere Love

The Bible encourages us to make sure our love is authentic. It tells us to have "sincere affection" for the brethren and to "love one another fervently from a pure heart" (1 Peter 1:22 AMPC). It also instructs us to make sure our love is not merely theory or speech, but is seen in our deeds "and in truth (in practice and in sincerity)" (1 John 3:18 AMPC).

I don't believe we think about the sincerity (authenticity) of our actions nearly as much as we should. We probably think if we are doing something, that is all that matters. But to God, what matters most is the motive behind the action. I urge you: Please take time to sincerely think about the importance of your motives and examine them carefully. The big question is, why are you doing what you are doing?

## Authenticity in Friendship

We all want friends who are genuine and authentic and who can be trusted. We want to believe that what they say to us is true, and they want the same from us. We do not want to think that our friends say good things to our face but bad things behind our back. Neither do we want to be concerned that our friends will tell our secrets to other people.

I have discovered through the study of God's Word and my own experience that we should treat other people the way we want to be treated. God's Word says that in the way we judge, we will be judged (Matthew 7:1–2), and if we are merciful, we will be shown mercy (Matthew 5:7). Jesus says, "Do to others what you would have them do to you" (Matthew 7:12). If we *want* authentic friends, let's be sure we *are* authentic friends.

> If we want *authentic friends, let's be sure we are authentic friends.*

The apostle James writes that out of the same mouth come blessing and cursing, and that this should never be the case (James 3:10). In other words, we are to avoid double-talk. He was referring to blessing God and then cursing or talking unkindly about people, but the idea can also be applied to being complimentary and kind to people's faces and then going away and speaking unkindly about them to others. Perhaps we noticed a flaw in them, and although we would not say anything to them about it, we delight in telling others. Would we want a friend to do that to us? No, of course not. Therefore, we should not do it to them.

A friend loves "at all times, and a brother is born for adversity" (Proverbs 17:17 KJV). True, genuine friends stick with us through hard times. About fifteen years ago, I allowed a major media outlet in our city to come to our office to do an extensive interview about our ministry, particularly the mission outreaches we are privileged to do in the United States and abroad. They also asked to come to one of our conferences to see what they were like. We were looking forward to the media release, because they had promised us it would be an honest and genuine report. However, when it came out, the information we shared was twisted, and we were made to look like greedy, dishonest people who could not be trusted. The only picture they showed from our conferences was an usher with an offering basket. I was devastated and can tell you that it was among the most painful events of my life.

They tried hard to damage our reputation, but God allowed the ministry to continue to grow during that time. No matter what people do, God will vindicate you if you continue trusting Him and are willing to forgive those who hurt you.

During that difficult time of public harassment, some of our partners dropped their partnership, and supposed friends never reached out even once with a word of encouragement. However, we also had others who let us know that they didn't believe any of the false stories, and they encouraged us. We also gained new partners. A true friend will stick with you not only when you are popular but also when you seem to be declining in popularity. Don't ever believe anything bad that you hear about anyone unless two or three reliable witnesses verify it (2 Corinthians 13:1). And even if you find it to be true, you don't need to spread it. I wish good news traveled as fast as bad news does, don't you?

Beware of people who are always spreading gossip, telling other people's secrets and even doing it under the pretense of "I'm just telling you this so you can pray." You can be sure that if someone is telling you other people's secrets, they are also telling yours.

After the incident with the media, I was strongly tempted to not trust anyone, but of course we can't live that way and have good, enjoyable relationships. We can, how-

> You can be sure that if someone is telling you other people's secrets, they are also telling yours.

ever, learn to be more discerning and cautious, and we can be on guard and careful about what we tell people, especially those we don't know very well.

## Authentic Friends Are Faithful

The biblical woman Ruth was a true friend to her mother-in-law, Naomi. Ruth refused to leave Naomi during hard times, even though it meant personal deprivation. Naomi's husband and two sons had died, leaving Naomi and her sons' wives (Ruth and Orpah) as widows in a foreign land (Ruth 1:1–5).

Naomi encouraged her two daughters-in-law to go back to their families so they would be taken care of, because she was poor and had nothing to offer them. One went home, but Ruth refused to leave Naomi (Ruth 1:16–17). Together they traveled to Israel, the land of Naomi's birth. They did face some hardship, but God gave Ruth favor with Boaz, a wealthy man in Israel. He provided food for them, and in the end, he and Ruth were married. Through that marriage, Ruth was included in the lineage of Jesus Christ (Matthew 1:5). God rewards faithfulness, and He delights in authentic people.

Elisha was a true friend to Elijah, refusing to leave him even though Elijah repeatedly told him to go (2 Kings 2:1–6). Elisha stayed with Elijah until the very end of his life, and God gave Elisha a double portion of Elijah's spirit (2 Kings 2:9–14). Elisha went on to become a great and powerful prophet.

When we are faithful to our friends, we not only bless those we befriend, but we also bless ourselves, because God will bless us for our faithfulness. Be sure you are a faithful friend and not a person who is only on board when everything benefits you and jumps ship when rough weather comes.

No matter how many people let you down, God will always stand by you. He will never leave you or forsake you (Hebrews 13:5). The apostle Paul had been a faithful leader and friend to many disciples, but at his first trial, everyone deserted him. He said that no one stood by him, and then he prayed that God would forgive them (2 Timothy 4:16). Wow! I think he understood that they were harming themselves more than they were harming him.

We may not see the word *authenticity* frequently in Scripture, but there is no doubt that in many ways, God's Word calls us to be authentic. As I have mentioned, it talks about having a pure heart (Psalm 24:3–5; Matthew 5:8), being genuine (Proverbs 21:21; 1 Timothy 1:5), telling the truth (Ephesians 4:25; Colossians 3:9), and living an honest life (Proverbs 6:16–20; 2 Corinthians 8:21). No matter how we may try to be like other people, most people can tell whether we are authentic or not. An authentic believer is a very powerful witness for God.

Let me encourage you today to make a decision to be an authentic, genuine, faithful friend. God will bless you for it!

CHAPTER 4

# Uniquely You

*You're born an original, don't die a copy!*

John Mason

Finding fault with ourselves is easy to do. People around us may be quick to point out our faults, and our enemy, the devil, certainly reminds us of them. But we do not have to believe everything other people or the enemy may say to us. We should compare everything we believe with God's Word to see if it is true or not. God created each of us, and according to Psalm 139, He did it very carefully. God doesn't make mistakes, and all of His works are wonderful. That means you are wonderful!

Yes, even with your faults God sees you as wonderful. He not only sees what you are doing now, but more importantly, He knows what you can and will do in the future as you allow Him to work with and in you. He sees the end from the beginning.

> I make known the end from the beginning, from ancient times, what is still to come. I say, "My purpose will stand, and I will do all that I please."
>
> Isaiah 46:10

God knows His will for you, and if you agree and cooperate with Him, it will come to pass. God's purposes always stand.

He has begun a good work in you, and He will bring it to completion (Philippians 1:6). Through your personal relationship with God and your study of His Word, you are continually growing spiritually and being transformed into the image of Jesus Christ.

In order to be your unique self, you must be willing to follow the guidance of the Holy Spirit that you sense in your heart rather than always looking to other people to tell you what to do. People are quick to give advice, but that doesn't mean that their advice is right for you. In some instances, taking advice is wise, but even then, we need to make sure it is wise and godly. God's Word tells us not to take counsel from the ungodly (Psalm 1:1).

## Let God Guide You

Instead of thinking you cannot hear from God or being fearful that you will somehow miss His guidance, be positive. Believe that you do hear from Him and that if you miss Him, He will find you. God meets us where we are and helps us get to where we should be. He can even take our mistakes and make them work out for our good as long as we keep trusting Him.

God is often a lot more confident in us than we are in ourselves, and He will never give up on us. When we fail or fall down, as long as we keep getting back up and trying again, God will keep working with us. Although we will have imperfections as long as we live, we do get stronger and improve all the time. Instead of thinking about how far we have to go, we should celebrate how far we have come.

When we need wisdom in any situation, we should ask God for it, and He will give it to us. He will guide us, according to James

1:5: "If any of you lacks wisdom, you should ask God, who gives generously to all without finding fault, and it will be given to you."

> *It is important to believe that something good will come out of our challenges.*

James 1 also teaches us how we should behave during trials and difficulties and what we should believe during those times. It is important to believe that something good will come out of our challenges. We are to persevere and trust God to give us wisdom when we ask for it. James writes that God gives generously and does so "without finding fault" with us, and I love that. Although we do have faults, and the trouble we find ourselves in may in some instances be due to those shortcomings, God does not reproach us or find fault with us when we ask Him for help and wisdom concerning how to handle the situations we encounter. He lovingly helps us! But when we ask, we need to ask in faith and not be double-minded, because doubt steals our faith. Make up your mind about what you believe about God and stand firm, no matter how your situation looks or how long it lasts.

> Since you are my rock and my fortress, for the sake of your name lead and guide me.
>
> Psalm 31:3

God doesn't help us because we deserve His assistance; He helps us for His name's sake. He has promised to answer when we call on Him, and He will never fail to do so. His name is connected with truth and goodness, and for the sake of His name, He can never do anything inconsistent with His nature. His answer may not be what we want to hear, but He *will* answer.

Whether you turn to the right or to the left, your ears will hear a voice behind you, saying, "This is the way; walk in it."

Isaiah 30:21

How do we hear God's voice? It is not usually an audible voice, but a still, small voice in our spirit that causes us to know what to do. Elijah made many attempts to hear from God in a time of turmoil in his life, but not until he got still and waited on God did he hear that beautiful "still, small voice" giving him direction (1 Kings 19:12 AMPC). The NIV says that he heard a "gentle whisper." Regardless of how it's translated, it was not a loud, booming, boisterous voice. It was quiet, and Elijah had to be still and quiet in order to hear it.

In order to be your unique self, it is important for you to know that you can be guided by God. He will put desires in your heart, and they may not make sense to anyone but you. This is why you can't let other people tell you what to do with your life. It is *your* life, given to you as a gift from God. He has gifted you in a way that will allow you to fit into His perfect plan, but only if you follow Him and refuse to let the demands and pressures of other people control you.

What do you do if your desire is to become a concert pianist, but your dad wants you to take over the family business? You should lovingly explain to him that if you take over the business, you won't do a good job because you have something else in your heart. People who don't follow their hearts are never happy. They live frustrated, disappointing lives.

*People who don't follow their hearts are never happy.*

Be courageous enough to be true to yourself, and the people who genuinely love you will stick with you even if you don't do what they think you should do.

Most people have a strong tendency to try to get other people to do what they are doing, the way they do it, but what God has led them to do may not work for other people. I recently talked with a man who heard from God about a way to discipline himself to have a regular devotional time. This man had previously had difficulty disciplining himself in this area, but when he did what God placed in his heart, it worked perfectly for him. He quickly found himself succeeding in an area in which he had previously failed. He immediately began telling other people that they should do what God told him to do, thinking that they would get the same positive result he enjoyed, but they didn't.

I believe it is a mistake to do something like this unless God has directed you to do so. We are all unique, and what works for one person may not work for another. Just as we don't like being pressured, neither do other people, so let's make sure we don't pressure others to do what we do. Making a suggestion is fine, but pressure is not a good idea. If you are talking with someone who is insecure, this person will feel compelled to do what you suggest and then be confused and may even feel condemned if it doesn't work. Help people find their own path in life instead of pressuring them to walk on your path.

> *Help people find their own path in life instead of pressuring them to walk on your path.*

## Relax and Be Who You Are

Ralph Waldo Emerson said, "To be yourself in a world that is constantly trying to make you someone else is the greatest accomplishment."

Trying to make others be what we want them to be or succumbing to their pressure to make us be what they want us to be is a major reason relationships fail. People must be free to be themselves, or they will always be frustrated, unfulfilled, and unable to relax and enjoy their life. They rarely know why they feel the way they do, so they blame their unhappiness on the people with whom they are in relationship.

Because I was abused sexually by my father, I always felt that something was wrong with me. That negative feeling drove me to try to be like other people I admired or thought I "should" be like. If anyone even suggested that I do something differently than the way I was doing it, I immediately felt pressure to change. Even if they were not trying to pressure me, the very idea that they didn't approve of what I was doing was enough to throw me into a panic.

Years later, after I was married and had children, I had a good friend who visited my house often. At times, she sat and talked with me while I did my ironing (yes, people once ironed all their clothes). One day she asked, "Why do you start with the collar of a shirt when you iron? I always start with the body."

My friend was simply making a comment, but from then on, when she was at my house and I was ironing, I started with the body of the shirt. I did what I thought would gain her approval instead of ironing the way that was comfortable for me. The funny thing is, she probably didn't even notice how I was ironing the shirt after her initial comment, so all my effort was wasted.

For a long time, I tried to be like so many people that I lost myself. Because I had rejected myself and viewed myself as flawed and useless, the idea that I could follow my own heart and trust God to guide me never occurred to me. I tried to be like my husband, who is the exact opposite of me. I tried to be like my pastor's wife, who was also the opposite of me. And I tried to be like a friend who had talents I didn't have. She had a garden and grew tomatoes and a few other vegetables, so I tried to have a garden. Of course, I failed at gardening. I failed in all of my pursuits to be like other people because God will never help anyone be someone else. He didn't create us to be copies of another person, but to be our own authentic and unique selves.

During those years, I blamed everyone else for my unhappiness and thought that if they would just change, I would be happy. Thankfully, God showed me the real problem—self-rejection, self-blame, guilt, and comparison. Only after I learned that I could accept and love myself because God accepts and loves me was I able to begin being the unique person He created me to be without comparing myself to others.

I can remember a time when I would walk into a room filled with people and immediately feel pressure from the fear of rejection. I would locate the person in the room who seemed to be getting the most attention and imitate them or get close to them so I could be accepted. Living like an impostor is exhausting, and I am so glad to be able to walk into any room now and feel no need to impress anyone. I thoroughly enjoy the freedom to be myself. If you have not yet reached that place, hopefully you will learn some lessons in this book that will help you get there. We are never truly free until we no longer feel the need to impress other people and can be comfortable just being ourselves.

Just think about this for a while. You never get away from yourself for one second of your life. Anywhere you go, there you are! If you don't like yourself, you are destined for a life of misery. All you have to do is think about how miserable it is to spend a few hours with someone you really don't enjoy, and you will begin to understand how being with yourself

> *If you don't like yourself, you are destined for a life of misery.*

all the time affects you if you don't enjoy yourself. If you don't like yourself, it affects every area of your life and every decision that you make.

If you don't like yourself and love yourself as God loves you, you are only one step away from freedom—a step of faith. It is a step you can take right now by simply believing that God's Word is true and that it is true *for you*. What you believe is your reality. Whatever you think you are is what you will become. For example, if I believe I am unlovable, I will behave in a way that makes me unlovable. However, if I believe I am lovable, I will behave in ways that draw people to me, and God will give me favor with them. Take some time and really examine how you feel and what you believe about yourself. You can never get where you want to be if you don't recognize where you are.

## Agree with God

How can two people walk together unless they have agreed to do so (Amos 3:3)? We cannot walk with God unless we make a decision to agree with Him about everything He says. This is a decision we make willfully. If you have not already made that decision, you can do so right now.

The Merriam-Webster online dictionary says that part of the definition of the word *accept* is "to receive (something offered) willingly." God offers us acceptance, and we can use our will to make a decision to receive that acceptance right now and every day that we live. He never rejects us, and He even says in His Word that those who do reject us are actually rejecting Him (Luke 10:16).

Let me urge you to agree with God that when He created you, He created something good.

> And God saw everything that He had made, and behold, it was very good (suitable, pleasant) and He approved it completely. And there was evening and there was morning, a sixth day.
>
> Genesis 1:31 AMPC

God had written every day of our lives in His book before even one of them existed (Psalm 139:16). This means that He not only saw the good we would do, but He also saw every sin and mistake we would commit and every flaw and weakness we would have—and He still accepts and loves us. Agree with God right now and accept yourself.

> *When God created you, He created something good.*

Self-rejection does not help you change; it actually multiplies your misery. Accepting yourself where you are and asking God to make you what He wants you to be is the way He wants you to approach your relationship with Him.

God told Jeremiah that before He formed him in the womb, He knew and approved of him as His "chosen instrument" (Jeremiah 1:5 AMPC). Surely, Jeremiah made mistakes and was far from perfect, but God saw his heart. A perfect heart in someone who makes mistakes is more important to God than a good performance that comes from an impure heart. All God wants is for us to love Him and admit our sins, and He is quick to forgive us and remember our sins no more (Hebrews 8:12).

## Accepting Correction Brings Change

God accepts us as we are and then goes about the work of changing us to be the best version of ourselves that we can be. This is a gentle and timely work, and it usually requires correction.

The Lord disciplines the one he loves, and he chastens everyone he accepts as his son.

Hebrews 12:6

God corrects us out of His love for us. I am thankful that He loves me too much to leave me as I am, and I hope you feel the same way. He helps us improve and become more like Him a little bit at a time. He welcomes us to His heart and cherishes us. His methods of discipline and correction are perfect, and His timing is also always perfect. He reveals things to us about ourselves when we are ready to receive them and ready to change.

I did something last night that offended someone, and I knew right away that God was displeased with my behavior. I apologized to the person I hurt, but I knew God would still deal with me about the situation. This wasn't the first time He had corrected me about a similar incident. Sometimes my mouth moves faster than my brain, and I speak harshly. Although I don't intend to offend or hurt people, I do. I could say, "Well, they shouldn't get offended!" However, I must take responsibility for my wrong actions and ask God not only to forgive me but also to change me.

What do I mean when I say that God "would deal with me" about the situation? I mean that I could feel His chastisement in my spirit, but at the same time I felt His love. I appreciate His caring enough about me to keep correcting me about this until the change in me is complete.

I haven't always been so accepting or positive about God's correction. There was a time when I took it as rejection instead of direction, and I felt condemned instead of lovingly corrected. That, of course, was my fault, not God's, and I felt that way because I was filled with self-rejection and had no revelation of how much God loves me.

Realizing that God's love is unconditional and everlasting is life-changing. There is never one moment in your life when God doesn't love you. He may not love

> *There is never one moment in your life when God doesn't love you.*

everything you do, but He never stops loving you.

I strongly encourage you to accept God's correction with appreciation, knowing that He corrects you only because He loves you. Accepting His correction joyfully is what brings change in you. His Holy Spirit lives in you as a believer in Jesus Christ. He deals with you from the inside out, not from the outside in, as the world does. God deals with your heart and causes you to want to be what He wants you to be. Then, because you want what He wants, He can change you.

We cannot change by self-effort or self-discipline alone. We need God's help. His work in us is spiritual; it begins in our spirit through the work of the Holy Spirit, and all the praise and credit goes to God, not to us.

Invite God to work in you, bringing correction in His way and time. When He does, accept it joyfully and thank Him for loving you enough to keep working with you to make you more like Jesus.

> *Invite God to work in you, bringing correction in His way and time.*

# CHAPTER 5

# You Are Exceptional

*For nothing will be impossible with God.*

Luke 1:37 ESV

Countless passages and stories about God's people in His Word let us know that we are exceptional, if for no other reason than that we belong to God. To be exceptional means to be outstanding and beyond ordinary, and I believe that every child of God—including you—fits that description.

God's Spirit lives in us, and nothing is impossible with Him (Luke 1:37).

*We are full of possibilities.*

We are full of possibilities. We cannot comprehend how great our lives can be with God, because the possibilities are limitless.

God told a man named Abram (later Abraham) that He would make of him a great nation, that He would bless him and make his name great, and that he would be a blessing to others (Genesis 12:2). Abraham was an ordinary man, but when God called him to do something extraordinary, he stepped out in faith to do it. Although he went through many difficult years that tested his faith greatly, he saw God keep His promise, and this ordinary man became the father of many nations and the father of faith in God, an example for others to follow.

I want to motivate you to be excited about your future and to believe that your possibilities know no bounds in God. God can give you skills that you do not currently possess. He can enable you to do things far beyond anything you could ever imagine yourself doing. He can give you favor with people who can open doors of opportunity for you. Dream big and ask God for great things, because He is "able to do immeasurably more than all we ask or imagine" (Ephesians 3:20).

Don't be concerned about your weaknesses, because they won't stop God. His strength shines brightest and is made perfect in your weaknesses (2 Corinthians 12:9). God created everything we see out of nothing, so just imagine what He can do with even the smallest thing you give Him.

## Offer Yourself to God

I want to encourage you to give everything you are—and everything you are not—to God to use as He pleases. Paul instructed the Romans to offer "your bodies [presenting all your members and faculties] as a living sacrifice" to God (Romans 12:1 AMPC). (In this verse, the word *faculties* refers to your abilities.) I had often heard preachers say that we should give all that we are to God, but He spoke to my heart one day about Romans 12:1 and told me to also give Him all that I am not, meaning my weaknesses, because He could use them too. He chooses the weak and "foolish things of the world to confound the wise" (1 Corinthians 1:27 KJV).

There was a time when I had some serious health problems and was very weak. I experienced excessive bleeding and had to have a hysterectomy. I took estrogen to make up for the estrogen my body no longer produced and was doing fairly well. But then I was diagnosed with breast cancer and had to have a mastectomy on the right side. Thankfully, I didn't have to take chemotherapy or radiation because the cancer cells had not reached my lymph nodes, but I wasn't able to take estrogen any longer because the tumor I had was estrogen-dependent.

The hysterectomy sent me into the change of life suddenly when I was in my early forties. I had to go through that transition without the support of hormones, and I was also working very hard because the ministry was fairly new and growing rapidly. At times I was so tired that I felt I could not go on. But I kept putting one foot in front of the other, and God gave me strength for each day. One morning I got up and felt especially bad. I went onto my deck to pray, and I recall telling God, "I don't have much energy left, Lord, but whatever I have, I give it to You for You to use as You desire." I didn't feel that what I had was enough to do very much, but He took what I gave Him and did extraordinary things.

Over the next several years, God did great things, including giving me the opportunity to begin teaching His Word on television. If you will give God whatever you have, no matter how little it is, He can do something wonderful with it. Remember, Jesus fed five thousand people with nothing more than a little boy's lunch (Matthew 14:13–21).

Complete surrender to God gives you great power. Our enemy, the devil, hates progress of any kind, but as we give ourselves completely to God, He gives us power to defeat the enemy. God's Word says, "So give yourselves completely to God. Stand against the devil, and the devil will run from you" (James 4:7 NCV). This is a wonderful scripture. The devil tries to give everyone trouble, especially those who are moving forward in their relationship with God, but complete surrender gives us power over him.

## God Qualifies Us for His Use

You don't have to be qualified in your natural state for God to use you in an extraordinary way; you simply have to be available and surrendered to Him. In the New Testament, Dorcas was a seamstress, and she was raised from the dead. Luke was a doctor, Peter was a fisherman, and Matthew was a tax collector—and Jesus chose them as His disciples, who shared His ministry on earth and helped carry the gospel message to the world after His death and resurrection. Mary Magdalene, who was believed to have been a prostitute, suffered the torment of seven demons until Jesus set her free from them. After her salvation and deliverance, she traveled with a group of women who supported Jesus' ministry and helped in the work of spreading the gospel.

These ordinary people did extraordinary feats. For years, I was a stay-at-home mom with only a high school education who sometimes worked as an office clerk. I had no speaking experience or education in the area of public speaking or Bible teaching, no one to mentor me, and no money. My friends told me I had the wrong personality for leading a ministry. In addition, I was convinced my deep voice would be a hindrance. When God called me to be in ministry, very few women functioned in such a role. In the natural realm, everything was against me. But God was for me, and that is all anyone needs to be a success. If you will step out in faith in obedience to God, He will guide you one step at a time.

God's anointing—His presence, ability, and power, which enables us to do certain things—qualifies and equips us. Even if we could do certain things naturally without God's anointing, our abilities become much more effective with His presence and power. For example, a person might have a beautiful voice that people enjoy hearing, but if God anoints that voice to sing for Him, it will affect people differently than singing without His anointing. Two people can teach the same message from the Bible word for word, but if one is anointed to do it and one isn't, the message from the anointed one will have a much deeper and more profound impact.

It is God's anointing that destroys the yoke of bondage in people's lives (Isaiah 10:27). When someone who is anointed to teach God's Word teaches it, people are set free from lies and deceptions that previously held them captive.

Jesus was called the "Anointed One" (Mark 8:29; Acts 26:23; Ephesians 4:15 AMPC). We don't hear as much as we should about the anointing. The words *anoint* and *anointing* are used many times in the Bible. In the Old Testament, prophets, priests, and kings were anointed with oil for the offices in which they stood. This oil represented the Holy Spirit's enabling presence and power that would come upon them, setting them apart for the job they were called to do. In the New Testament, all believers are anointed with the Holy Spirit, who gives us power and ability to do extraordinary things for the glory of God.

Speaking to all believers, the apostle John says,

> But you have an anointing from the Holy One, and all of you know the truth.
>
> 1 John 2:20

> As for you, the anointing you received from him remains in you, and you do not need anyone to teach you. But as his anointing teaches you about all things and as that anointing is real, not counterfeit—just as it has taught you, remain in him.
>
> 1 John 2:27

First John 2:27 doesn't mean that we no longer need the gift of
the teacher in the church. It does mean that we don't need others
to continually tell us what to do because God will teach us by His
anointing. His anointing guides us and teaches us. Even when a
Bible teacher is teaching the Word, it is the anointing of the Holy
Spirit that helps us understand it.

We all need God's anointing. Even Jesus was anointed for His
ministry. He said,

> The Spirit of the Lord is on me, because he has anointed
> me to proclaim good news to the poor. He has sent me to
> proclaim freedom for the prisoners and recovery of sight
> for the blind, to set the oppressed free, to proclaim the
> year of the Lord's favor.
>
> Luke 4:18–19

God not only anoints people to
do ministry, but He anoints people
to do all kinds of things. One can be
anointed by God to encourage oth-

*Anointing is what makes us exceptional.*

ers, to help them, to show mercy, or to teach (Romans 12:4–8).
Some are anointed in the area of organizational skills, business,
leadership, or musical ability. The important point to remember
is that even if we are not naturally qualified to do something specific, God can qualify us with His anointing if doing it is His will
for us. As a matter of fact, if we try to operate by natural skills
alone, we may do something, but it won't be what it could be
with God's help. We need God's anointing, no matter what area
of service we want to work in. This anointing is what makes us
exceptional.

## Nothing Is Too Small for God to Use in a Big Way

Is the saying "The bigger, the better" accurate? I don't think so. God takes the little things we give Him or do for Him, and He does great things with them. Dwight L. Moody said, "There are many of us that are willing to do great things for the Lord, but few of us are willing to do little things."

I believe that anyone who wants to do great things for the Lord will be tested. The first tests often involve needing to be faithful in little things.

> Whoever can be trusted with very little can also be trusted with much, and whoever is dishonest with very little will also be dishonest with much.
>
> Luke 16:10

I was definitely tested by needing to stay faithful to do little things well before I was promoted to do greater things. I quit my job in order to study for the ministry I believed I would one day have. That step of obedience left us a little short of being able to pay our bills each month. In addition, we had nothing for any repairs, clothes, or unexpected expenses. It was a huge step of faith and I was afraid, but I knew it was what God wanted, so He gave me the grace to do it.

I taught a Bible study of twelve women for a few months at breakfast meetings in a restaurant. Then our Bible study moved from the restaurant to my home, and it grew to twenty-five to thirty people each Tuesday evening and stayed at that number for five years. During that time, I received no pay. Some people did occasionally give me an offering, which was badly needed. When I look back now, I can say it was totally amazing how God took care of our financial needs. We never knew where His provision would come from. But He always provided and that helped us to grow in our faith.

After I stopped doing the Bible study because I felt God led me to discontinue it, I did nothing for a year. Then I started attending a new church, and the leaders there asked me to lead a women's Bible study group. It began with 110 ladies and grew over a period of five years from 110 to 400–500 ladies. My starting salary was $65 a week, and I was thrilled. While on staff at that church, in addition to the weekly women's Bible study, I also had the privilege of teaching in a Bible school three times a week and teaching in the main church service often when the pastor was out of town. I was gaining experience while I was faithfully working in someone else's ministry for five years. I did anything I was asked to do, but I also had a deep desire and sense of calling to build my own ministry.

Then, once again, I felt God leading me to make a change, so I left my position at the church and began broadcasting a fifteen-minute program on several radio stations. I also taught in some weekly meetings in the St. Louis area. After a while, our ministry began to grow, but it happened very slowly. We did hundreds of meetings of fewer than one hundred people, but I prepared and taught as though there were ten thousand people in attendance. Those meetings gradually grew, and eventually we went on television once a week and then, after a while, expanded to daily television. Then we began having conferences in hotel ballrooms, then larger meeting rooms, and finally arenas. Our ministry spread outside of the United States and is now broadcast around the globe in more than one hundred languages. I have been privileged to take sixty-seven mission trips, including conferences, and to minister in a variety of ways to the beautiful people in the countries we traveled to.

We have also been privileged to fund outreaches to the poor; build orphanages; dig more than one thousand clean water wells; build schools, hospitals, and medical clinics; and send more than three million of my books into prison cells. We have distributed sixty million books around the world in more than one hundred languages. All of this may sound impressive to you, but it has taken forty-five years, and to me they have felt like forty-five very long years, with a lot of hard work and waiting periods in between each growth spurt. Many times I had to read and reread Zechariah 4:10, which encourages us not to despise the small beginnings because God rejoices to see the work begin. He simply wants us to get started in obedience to His call.

When we think about Jesus, we think about all of the great miracles He performed, but He also did a lot of small things. He washed the disciples' feet (John 13:4–5), and He cooked them breakfast (John 21:9). His first miracle was turning water into wine to make a wedding feast turn out well (John 2:1–11). He stopped during His travels to help anyone who asked Him, no matter who they were. We often study the steps of Jesus, but perhaps we should study the "stops" of Jesus. We are often too busy being religious to stop and help those in need, but Jesus wasn't.

Jesus noticed Zacchaeus, a hated tax collector, perched in a tree trying to see Him, and went to his house for dinner (Luke 19:1–5). He saw the rich putting their offerings into the temple treasury, and He saw the widow who put in two small copper coins—less than a penny's worth in today's money (Luke 21:1–4). He said she had done a great thing. The rich gave some out of their abundance, but the poor widow gave all she had. She is still being preached about more than two thousand years later. Jesus didn't look at the amount she gave, but at the sacrifice she made.

Jesus wept over the unbelief and pain in the world (John 11:35).

He made His triumphal entry into Jerusalem on a donkey (Matthew 21:1–10). The donkey was not a very impressive animal, but the act of humility still amazes us today. I'm pretty sure I would have chosen a white stallion wearing bejeweled tack. What about you?

No matter how little you have or think you can do, offer it to God, and He will do great things. If you are faithful over a little, you will be made ruler over much (Matthew 25:23). You are exceptional, and you will do extraordinary things because all things are possible with God.

# CHAPTER 6

# If at First You Don't Succeed, You're Normal!

*Only those who dare to fail greatly can ever achieve greatly.*
Robert F. Kennedy

We can easily embrace and approve of ourselves when we succeed, but what about when we fail? When we try something and it doesn't work, are we still able to embrace and approve of ourselves? If not, then we will never enjoy emotional stability because our opinion of ourselves will change based on how well we are or are not doing each day.

I would venture to say that most people who have accomplished great things have failed many times on their way to success. According to various sources, Thomas Edison said he failed his way to success. I have heard and read on several occasions that he made approximately two thousand attempts to invent the light bulb, and failed repeatedly before he succeeded. Now, though, when you ask people who invented the light bulb, they will say, "Thomas Edison." He is remembered for his success, not his failures.

Sometimes our mistakes can be turned into something useful. Ivory soap was not supposed to float, but because of a manufacturing error, it did. That mistake became its greatest selling point. The material used to manufacture Kleenex tissues was originally invented as a gas-mask filter during World War I. It later failed as a cold cream remover, but finally hit upon success when it was repackaged as a disposable handkerchief. Now Americans buy nearly 200 billion tissues a year.

I appreciate these stories and have included them in several of my books because they remind me of the way God has taken many of my mistakes and turned them into life lessons and illustrations I can use to teach other people. I often say that I have learned a great deal from my mistakes and from watching the mistakes of others. We all make mistakes, and at times we fail at what we try to do. But God can make miracles out of mistakes. The way we react to failures is much more important than the failures themselves.

I read that 80 to 90 percent of all product launches fail, which shows us we need not be afraid of failure. Failing at something doesn't make

> God can make miracles out of mistakes.

you a failure; the only way you can fail is to quit trying. Anyone can overcome a failure, but not everybody chooses to overcome a bad attitude about those failures.

John Maxwell says that we can "fail forward," and it is true. We can learn from our mistakes, but not until we stop feeling guilty about them. Our mistakes bother us a lot more than they bother God because He knew that we would make them before He ever created

> Our mistakes bother us a lot more than they bother God.

us. Failure isn't final, and it's not fatal; it is part of the human condition. If you make mistakes, you are normal. If we made no mistakes, we wouldn't need Jesus.

## God Uses People Who Fail

As long as we are willing to get back up after we fall down, God will keep working with us until we have success. God's Word states that a righteous person falls down seven times and gets up again (Proverbs 24:16). I'm way past seven times, so I'm very glad that God is merciful.

The Bible is filled with stories of people who failed miserably and ended up being used by God greatly. Think, for example, about the prophet Elijah. He experienced great victories, but he also struggled with deep depression. Elijah had prophesied that there would be no rain for several years, and there was not. After three dry years, God told him to present himself to King Ahab and that when he did, He would send rain. But before He did, something remarkable took place.

In an epic showdown between the power of a false god and the power of the one true God, Elijah told Ahab to assemble all the prophets of the false god Baal on Mount Carmel. When they met with Elijah there, he challenged them to build an altar, put wood on it, cut a bull into pieces, and call on their god to send the fire needed for the sacrifice. They cried out to their god, and nothing happened. But when Elijah did the same and cried to the Lord God Almighty, the one true God, fire came down from heaven and burned up the sacrifice. Elijah then executed all 450 of the false prophets of Baal (1 Kings 17:1; 18:1–40).

Just imagine how exhausted Elijah must have been that day! After God humiliated the prophets of Baal and revealed Himself through the fire on the altar, Elijah told Ahab to expect rain. After Elijah prayed seven times on Mount Carmel, a cloud appeared in the sky, and soon a great rain began to fall. He ran ahead of Ahab for a distance of about twenty miles, from Mount Carmel back into the city of Jezreel, where Ahab's palace was. This was all in a day's work for Elijah. (I'm impressed!)

But the next day, Ahab told his wife, Jezebel, how Elijah had killed her prophets. When she sent word that she was going to kill him, he ran into the wilderness and hid from her in fear. He finally sat under a tree and prayed to die (1 Kings 18:41–19:4).

Elijah went from being greatly elated one day before because of his success against the prophets of Baal to being deeply depressed and hiding in fear because of one woman the next. He succeeded and then he failed, but when we think of Elijah, we think of him as one of the greatest prophets that ever lived. We don't think of Elijah as a failure.

We know that King David failed God by committing adultery and murder, but he eventually repented, and God still favored David and used him mightily (2 Samuel 11:2–12:13; Acts 13:22).

John Mark was a deserter. He had traveled with Paul and Barnabas, and at some point got tired of it and just quit. We don't know why he deserted, but we do know his leaving was not honorable. A few years later, Barnabas suggested to Paul that they stop by John Mark's house and take him with them on their journey. We don't know the details of the story, but we must assume there had been some kind of repentance in order for Barnabas to do this. Paul didn't agree with Barnabas, and the disagreement was so intense that it caused them to separate (Acts 13:13; 15:37–40). However, years later, Paul wrote to the Colossians from prison and mentioned that John Mark was with him and had been a great comfort to him (Colossians 4:10–11). John Mark failed Paul, but their relationship was eventually restored completely.

We know that Peter denied Jesus three times (Luke 22:61), yet God still used him greatly. Moses failed by letting his anger control him at times (Exodus 11:8; 32:19), but God performed mighty signs and wonders through him (Deuteronomy 34:10–12). Paul had persecuted and hunted down Christians to be imprisoned (Acts 8:3; Galatians 1:13), yet God chose him by His grace to write two-thirds of the New Testament and take the gospel to the Gentiles as well as Jews. Ruth was part of the lineage of Jesus Christ but had formerly been a Moabite who worshipped false gods (Matthew 1:5; Ruth 1:16–22). Thank God that the way we begin in life is not the way we have to end. He loves new beginnings.

## Inspiring Stories

Many people have faced rejection and experienced failure before they ever enjoyed success. Some of them, such as the ones whose stories I've included below, are quite recognizable.

### Abraham Lincoln

In the face of many defeats, Abraham Lincoln had reason to believe there was no way he could succeed in life or be president of the United States. At twenty-two years old, he failed in business. One year later, he ran for the legislature and lost. When he was twenty-four, he experienced a second business failure. At twenty-six, the woman he loved passed away, and he suffered a nervous breakdown the next year. When he was twenty-nine, he lost another political race, and at thirty-four he made an unsuccessful run for Congress. At thirty-seven, he did get elected to Congress, only to be defeated again two years later. At forty-six, he lost his bid for the Senate, and the next year, he failed in his attempt to become vice president. When he was forty-nine, he was defeated for the Senate again. He had four sons, but only one lived to adulthood. But, at fifty-one years of age, Abraham Lincoln was elected president of the United States, and he successfully led the country through one of its most difficult periods. Many people would have said "No way," but not Lincoln. He never gave up.

## Walt Disney

One of the most creative geniuses of the twentieth century was once fired from a newspaper because he was told he lacked creativity. Trying to persevere, Disney formed his first animation company, which was called Laugh-O-Gram Films. He raised $15,000 for the company but eventually was forced to close Laugh-O-Gram, following the close of an important distributor partner.

Desperate and out of money, Disney found his way to Hollywood and faced even more criticism and failure, until finally his first few classic films started to skyrocket in popularity.

## Milton Hershey

Everyone knows Hershey's chocolate, but when Milton Hershey first started his candy production career, he was a nobody. After being fired from an apprenticeship with a printer, Hershey started three separate candy-related ventures and was forced to watch all of them fail.

In one last attempt, Hershey founded the Lancaster Caramel Company and started seeing enormous results. Believing in his vision for milk chocolate for the masses, he eventually founded the Hershey Company and established a well-known name in the industry.

Let me encourage you to draw inspiration from these stories the next time you experience failure, no matter the scale. In the moment, some failure might seem like the end of the road, but remember, there are countless successful men and women in the world today who are enjoying success only because they decided to push past the inevitable bleakness of failure.

Learn from your mistakes, reflect on and accept your failures, but revisit your passion and keep pursuing your goals no matter what.

These few stories are among the thousands upon thousands of accounts of people who refused to give up and overcame failure to become extremely successful. You can do the same.

## A New Perspective on Failure

Why are some people so reluctant to try new things? I think we often stay in what we consider a safe zone because we care too much about what others think of us or what they might say to or about us. We want approval, and we risk not getting it if we try something and fail. Word of our failures certainly spreads faster than word of our successes. Knowing that we rarely get to fail privately often prevents us from taking chances we may want or need to take.

We need a new perspective on failure. First, let us realize that failure is not nearly as bad as we have convinced ourselves it is. How we perceive what happens in our lives becomes our reality, and all of us can change our perception. If you think about it seriously, you will see that allowing other people's thoughts to control your decisions often leads to immeasurable loss. After all, the life God gives you is your life, and it is the only one for which you will be asked to give an account when your time on Earth is finished.

So then, each of us will give an account of ourselves to God.

Romans 14:12

We often hear the phrase *they say* and go on to repeat what "they" say, but who are "they"? I realized a long time ago that we are in danger of letting the elusive "they" run our lives, and we don't even know who they are. Sometimes, they have no real interest in us and base their opinions on their own thoughts and ideas. At other times, we know who they are, and we need to ask ourselves whether they truly know what they are talking about or merely want to control us. When people love us with real, genuine love, that love sets us free and encourages us to follow our hearts and try to do things without fear of failure. It never threatens to reject us if we don't do as others would have us do.

We have all probably failed a few times trying to learn to do the things we now do quite easily. For example:

- As a toddler, did you suddenly begin walking without experiencing a fall while learning to do it?
- Did you learn to ride a bike without falling a few times?
- When you learned to roller skate, did you fall down a few times?
- Did you pass your driver's test the first time you took it? Perhaps you did, but many people do not, and I was one of them.
- Are you able to write a text, email, or article on your computer without having to correct even one mistake?

We don't seem to mind failures such as these because other people make them also. But when we fail as we try to do something unique or something people would not expect us to do, we become more careful. Being careful is wise, but it can become devastating when it turns into fear if that fear prevents us from taking action.

You owe it to yourself to try to be the best version you can be of yourself. Consider these questions:

- What is it that you want to do with or in your life that you have not yet done?
- Do you love your work, or would you really like to try something else?
- Do you love your life, or do you waste your time wishing you had someone else's existence? Are you tired of hearing other people's stories of the adventures they have had, and do you long for adventures of your own? Those adventures won't come to you; you must choose them.
- Do you long to have a new hairstyle but are concerned the new one might not be as good as the old one? You will never find out unless you step out and try it. What if your friends don't like it? What if you don't even like it?

We let what-if talk us out of following our heart's desires. It's time to stop that and start living the life you desire to live.

## Eight Ways to Develop a New Mindset

Gaining a new perspective requires a new way of thinking about yourself and your life. Here are eight suggestions to help you develop a new mindset.

## 1. Let go of perfection.

Nothing and no one is perfect except Jesus. We can have a perfect heart toward Him, but our performance will always be flawed to some degree because we are human. I have known perfectionists who annoy and frustrate themselves and everyone around them with their obsessive attention to details most people don't even see. They frequently fear failure and often live small lives because they spend excessive amounts of time on their failures instead of letting them go and pressing on to success.

## 2. Get to know yourself.

Truly knowing yourself—not simply believing what other people say about you—is a key to both authentic living and to personal fulfillment. If you want to know yourself better, consider these questions:

- What do you want out of life?
- What would you pursue or enjoy if you were not concerned at all about what others would think or say?
- Have you tried to be like others for so long that you have lost sight of what you want? If so, you can recapture your dreams.

## 3. Allow yourself to be vulnerable.

Take a chance on revealing the real you, and know that if you are rejected, you will survive. Going against the norm, trying something new, or facing disapproval can be terrifying, but you cannot succeed unless you take a chance on failing.

## 4. Stop hiding.

It is time to come out of hiding and be the person you truly want to be. It is time to be true to your own heart. You are beautiful, and it is time to let everyone see it. You have a gift to share with the world, and if you hide it due to fear of failure, we will all miss something that only you could have given us.

*You cannot succeed unless you take a chance on failing.*

## 5. Be your own best friend.

Give yourself a hug and decide to be kind to yourself. Remember that God has made you and that He doesn't make mistakes. If you like yourself, you don't have to be around people excessively, because you enjoy spending time with yourself. If people do reject you, it may not be pleasant or enjoyable, but it won't be nearly as devastating as it would be if you didn't like yourself.

## 6. Find your own group.

Pray for and look for people you are comfortable with, who are secure enough to let you be yourself. Find people with whom you can exchange ideas and who allow you to be original without judging you. Stay away from those who are critical and who easily find fault with others.

## 7. Ask for help.

Ask God for guidance and believe that He gives it. Ask others for help when you need it without letting those requests make you feel weak. We all need each other. We can do so much more together than we can ever do alone. I began my ministry by myself, but in order for it to become a ministry covering the Earth with God's Word, I needed hundreds of people—people who could do things that I could not do—to help me.

## 8. Doubt your doubts.

Doubt comes to all of us, but it usually does not offer good advice. Think very carefully and prayerfully about the decisions you want to make, and then stick with them. If you fall into the trap of self-doubt, you may end up being unsure about everything you want to do. If you make a decision and lose your peace about it, slow down and wait until you determine what is right. God guides us by peace, but our enemy the devil tries to guide us by fear and doubt.

If you never give up, you will eventually find your sweet spot. As you search for it, remember that failing at something doesn't make you a failure.

# CHAPTER 7

# What's Right with You?

*God made him who had no sin to be sin for us, so that in him we might become the righteousness of God.*

2 Corinthians 5:21

You have just read about the fact that everyone experiences failure and has weaknesses. This is true, but as I mentioned, failing does not make you a failure. There is a greater truth than the fact that you will fail at times, which is that *through Christ, no matter how you may fail or what your weaknesses may be, you are still righteous in God's sight.*

I want you to pay particular attention to this chapter, because if you don't understand what the phrase *the righteousness of God through Christ* means, then grasping God's love, approval, and acceptance and the freedom we have in and through Him will be very difficult—if not impossible—for you.

The devil's desire is to make you think and feel as though something is always wrong with you. Being sexually abused by my father caused a certain message to play incessantly in my head day after day for more than forty years of my life: "What is wrong with me?" I knew that what my father did to me was wrong, even though he told me that it was good and that he did it because he loved me and I was special. Knowing that his actions against me were wrong was good, but thinking something was wrong with me because of what he did was a huge problem.

Many people who are mistreated think the treatment they receive is their fault. Battered women often think it is their fault that their husband hits or beats them, so they try to be better and to make fewer mistakes so that their abusive partners don't become angry. However, ultimately the same pattern keeps repeating itself. *Abuse is not the mistreated person's fault.* The abuser has a problem and needs help.

Many children who are given up for adoption spend their lives wondering what was wrong with them to cause their birth parents not to want them. The ideas they come up with in their minds are often very far removed from the truth. The parent may not have been able to care for them and thought they were doing the best for them by letting someone who could give them a better life adopt them.

The thought *What is wrong with me?* is a core reason many become people-pleasers and approval addicts, become insecure, and lack confidence. As long as we are stuck in the mindset that something is wrong with us, we will feel guilty and be dysfunctional.

I think it is interesting that one of the first gifts God wants to give us after salvation is righteousness. He wants us to know there is a great deal right with us through our belief in and relationship with Jesus. God views us as being in right standing with Him because of our faith in Jesus Christ.

Receiving right standing with God by faith gives us joy, and according to Romans 5:1–2, it also produces peace. It is impossible to enjoy life if we feel "wrong" all the time.

## You Can't Earn God's Acceptance

Righteousness comes through faith, not keeping all the rules of religion. God does not play favorites or make distinctions, so this amazing righteousness is available to all. To qualify for God's righteousness we need to meet two requirements: We must sin, and we must believe in Jesus as the acceptable sacrifice for our sins.

> For all have sinned and fall short of the glory of God, and all are justified freely by his grace through the redemption that came by Christ Jesus.
>
> Romans 3:23–24

We rarely have any trouble believing that we are sinners. Believing we are justified freely by God's grace is often more difficult. Put most simply, to be justified means to be made just as though we had never sinned. *Nelson's New Illustrated Bible Dictionary* says that justification is "the process by which sinful human beings are made acceptable to a holy God. Christianity is unique because of its teaching of justification by grace" (see Romans 3:24). It goes on to say that justification is "based on the work of Christ, accomplished through His blood (Romans 5:9), and brought to His people through His resurrection" (see Romans 4:25).

*We rarely have any trouble believing that we are sinners. Believing we are justified freely by God's grace is often more difficult.*

We may read all about being made right with God through faith, but having righteousness become a reality to us usually takes some time. Our minds must be renewed to believe Christ has made us right with God. In addition, we must realize that no longer thinking something is wrong with us is perfectly acceptable to God. It is also perfectly acceptable to think something is right with us through Jesus while also being open to His conviction and correction.

The apostle Paul had been a Pharisee, a strict keeper of all the rules and regulations of the Jewish law, until he was gloriously saved by God's grace. He wanted to understand the right kind of righteousness and he prayed about this in Philippians 3:9:

> And be found in him, not having a righteousness of my own that comes from the law, but that which is through faith in Christ—the righteousness that comes from God on the basis of faith.

Although few Christians think they must abide by Old Testament rules and regulations, some are very good at making their own rules. Others may go to a church that makes rules for them to follow. Studying God's Word is one of the best investments of time and energy we can make, but we should never make a law out of doing it. If I miss a day studying my Bible, I don't have to feel guilty or wonder if God is displeased with me. We are encouraged to pray, but the New Testament offers no rules about praying except that we should do it. A pastor may say you should pray at least one hour a day, and their congregation may take that as a new rule they need to follow to be acceptable to God. But praying an hour each day is only the pastor's opinion; it is not based on Scripture. Jesus did say to His disciples when He was in the Garden of Gethsemane, "Couldn't you men keep watch with me for one hour?" (Matthew 26:40), but He was referring to that particular situation, not making a rule for all time and all people. An hour of prayer each day may be a good discipline, but it is not a law.

If I read a book for the purpose of learning more about a certain scriptural principle, I am still studying God's Word. Bible study doesn't mean I have to physically open a book with "The

Holy Bible" printed on the front cover in order to be studying God's Word. I can listen to Scripture, or to a sermon, or read a book, or meditate on Scripture, in addition to getting out my Bible and studying it. I find it good to take different approaches to our time in the Word on different days just for variety's sake. However, there are many people who begin their day by reading a specified number of chapters in their Bible. That is a wonderful habit also, but not a law.

When we turn anything we do into something we think we must do to earn credit with God or be acceptable to Him, we have lost sight of, or have never known, the true meaning of salvation through Christ.

We should do good works. The Word of God is clear on that subject, but it is also clear that our motive for doing them must not be to earn anything from God or to be well thought of by people. We do good works because of what Jesus has already done for us, not in order to get Him to do something for us. Good works are the natural fruit of our love for God and our faith in Him.

We trade our sin for God's righteousness. I call this "the great exchange." Through Jesus' sacrifice, we can exchange our ashes for beauty and our grief for the oil of joy. We receive praise in exchange for our depression, discouragement, despair, and sadness (Isaiah 61:3). We receive faith in exchange for our fear, and we receive freedom in Christ in exchange for our bondage (Luke 4:18; Romans 8:15; Hebrews 2:14–15).

## Joint-Heirs With Christ

Now if we are children, then we are heirs—heirs of God and co-heirs with Christ.

Romans 8:17

Everyone would love to receive an inheritance from a relative who has passed away. An inheritance is something we are freely given because someone loved us. We receive as a gift something that someone else earned. We may or may not have an inheritance from someone who loved us, but we all have an inheritance in Christ. This means that whatever Jesus receives from the Father because of His obedience to suffer and die in our place, we receive also by virtue of being "in Him" by faith. Just imagine it! In Christ, we inherit all that God has and is. I doubt we *can* imagine it. This spiritual truth is too wonderful for us to be able to fully grasp mentally, so we receive it by faith because God's Word teaches us that it is true.

I like to explain this using a personal example. When Dave and I married, I didn't have a car, but he did. I didn't have any money, but he did. Suddenly, when I said "I do," I had a car and money. I had done nothing right or wrong yet as his wife. I had simply received Dave as my husband for life and made a commitment to honor, obey, and love him in all circumstances and situations. Then, *bam*, everything he had became mine! Had I possessed anything, it would have become his, but I had nothing to offer besides myself, and Dave received me as I was. I was like we are when we come to Christ. We have nothing to offer Jesus when we come to Him except our sin and our life. He accepts what we have and gives us back forgiveness of sin, righteousness with God, and a life that is far better than the one we gave to Him.

When people sincerely offer themselves to God and believe that Jesus died for them and was raised from the dead, what happened to me when I married Dave happens to them on a much more profound scale. Everything God has is made available to them—not because they have anything to offer in exchange, but because God is good.

## Put On Righteousness

Ephesians 6:10–18 gives us some instructions on spiritual warfare, or how to defeat our enemy, the devil. Overcoming him is not as difficult as you might think. All we really need to do is wear the armor that God has supplied to every believer in Jesus. This armor consists of the "belt of truth," the "breastplate of righteousness," the "shield of faith," the shoes of "peace," the "helmet of salvation," and the "sword of the Spirit, which is the word of God." We then cover everything with all kinds of prayers at all times, in the Spirit.

Notice that these scriptures tell us that God supplies this armor, and then they give us instructions to put it on. Having something is one thing, while using it is quite another.

A simple explanation of these pieces of armor teaches us that we should know the truth, wear our righteousness (understand who we are in Christ), put on the helmet of salvation (think as a Christian should think), walk in peace, and approach everything in life in faith. In addition, we wield the sword of the Spirit by coming against the lies of Satan with the truth of God's Word. Lastly, we are to pray about absolutely everything.

What does it mean to "wear righteousness"? It means to know you are loved and are justified and in right standing with God. It does not mean overlooking sin or denying that you sin, but knowing that you are forgiven and have no need to feel guilty and condemned. It means you believe that you are made acceptable to God through your faith in Jesus Christ. It empowers you to be secure and confident, not insecure; to value yourself because God values you; and to recognize and embrace your uniqueness. Wearing righteousness sets you free to be authentic because you have become convinced that your worth and value are based not on what people think of you but on how God thinks toward you.

## Right Behavior

A peach tree produces peaches, and it does not have to struggle to do so. An apple tree produces apples, and it does not have to struggle to do so. Trees simply produce what they are. Similarly, righteous people produce right behavior, and they don't have to struggle to do so, because they yield the fruit of who they are. God never expects us to produce anything or be anything unless He first gives us the capability to do so. He makes us what He wants us to be. When we receive Jesus, we receive a new nature—the nature of God.

> God never expects us to produce anything or be anything unless He first gives us the capability to do so.

> Therefore if any person is [ingrafted] in Christ (the Messiah) he is a new creation (a new creature altogether); the old [previous moral and spiritual condition] has passed away. Behold, the fresh and new has come!
>
> 2 Corinthians 5:17 AMPC

New believers in Christ are full of wonderful possibilities. If they are bald, they don't suddenly grow hair, and if they have a bad temper, it does not immediately go away. What new believers do have are new possibilities. They become fresh new spiritual clay, and if they will allow the Holy Spirit to work with them, they will be transformed into the image of Jesus Christ.

I like to say that when we receive Christ, we receive the seed of God, spiritually speaking. We become pregnant, so to speak, with all that God is. We still must bring it to birth, and that takes time and patience.

Last night our son stopped by our house and showed Dave and me a photograph of himself as a baby lying belly down on Dave's chest. The first question I asked our son was, "Which one of your boys looks like you in that picture?" He named one right away.

We all want our children to look like us or to act like us, and God wants the same with us. He wants our behavior to imitate His. Jesus says, "Anyone who has seen me has seen the Father" (John 14:9). And we should be able to say, "If you have seen me, you have seen Jesus." We are His ambassadors as we represent Him (2 Corinthians 5:20).

Just as our children have our DNA in them, we have the Father's DNA, spiritually, in us. If we know we are right with Him, we will produce godly behavior. When we know who we are in Him, we don't have to strive to be good; we will produce goodness.

Once we know this, being a Christian is no longer a struggle. We don't exhaust ourselves trying to live as He would have us live. We simply go to Jesus and trust Him to bring out of us what He has put in us. The Holy Spirit lives in us (2 Timothy 1:14); therefore, we have all the fruit of the Holy Spirit in us. We simply need to learn to walk by the Spirit instead of by the flesh, and soon good fruit will be popping out everywhere.

Let me urge you: Stop trying to be something you already are. There is no need to struggle to be right when God's righteousness (rightness) has already been given to you through your faith in Jesus. Later in the book I will devote more material to righteousness, because it is one of the most important and valuable gifts God offers us, a gift we need to be sure we understand and receive.

*Stop trying to be something you already are.*

# CHAPTER 8

# Make Peace with Yourself

*If it is possible, as far as it depends on you, live at peace with everyone.*

Romans 12:18

Knowing that you are right with God should help you live at peace with yourself. In fact, God instructs us to "live at peace with everyone," and *everyone* includes ourselves. Let me ask you: Are you living at peace with yourself, or are you angry with yourself much of the time? Your quality of life partially depends on the type of relationship you have with yourself. You are with yourself more than anyone else you know, so you should learn to enjoy your own company.

Some people not only dislike themselves, but they actually hate themselves. Many years ago, I had a friend who had this problem. She was sad most of the time and easily angered. Her negative emotions were rooted in the way she felt about herself. The two of us once attended a church service in which the minister asked people who wanted prayer to come forward at the end of the service. My friend and I both responded. I've forgotten why I wanted prayer, but I distinctly remember what she wanted. The minister inquired about her request, and she said, "I hate myself." His response was very different than I would have expected. His facial expression became stern, and he asked her, "Who do you think you are?" I think we were both shocked. As we stood there he said, "Since Jesus loved you enough to suffer and die for you, the least you can do is like yourself!" His statement had a huge impact on me, and I've always remembered it. Our heavenly Father values us enough that He gave His only Son to pay for our sins and set us free from the guilt they cause us to feel. Knowing this—that God loves us so much—we should honor His sacrifice by being at peace with ourselves.

Making peace with yourself begins with thinking healthy, godly thoughts about who you are. Here is some advice to help you do this:

- Always reject and hate your sin, but don't reject or hate yourself.
- Be quick to repent of any and all sin.
- Be honest with God and with yourself about yourself.
- When God shows you something about yourself, don't be afraid of it.
- Stop making negative, disparaging comments about yourself, but don't boast, either.
- Don't have an exaggerated opinion of your own importance, but do not think you are insignificant.
- When something goes wrong, don't always assume it is your fault. But don't be too proud to admit it if you are wrong.
- Beware of having yourself on your mind too much. Don't meditate excessively on what you have done right or what you have done wrong. Both ways of thinking keep your mind on you! Keep your thoughts centered on God and His Word, and stay busy doing the good works He has predestined you to do (Ephesians 2:10). His Word teaches us that He will guard those and keep them in perfect peace, whose minds are stayed on Him (Isaiah 26:3).

- Take good care of yourself physically, and do the best you can with what God has given you to work with, but don't be excessively concerned or vain about your appearance.
- Learn all you can, but don't allow your education to become a point of pride. God does not use us merely because of our level of education, but because of our heart toward Him.
- Realize that your talents and abilities are gifts from God, not something you have managed to develop totally on your own. Don't look down on people who cannot do what you can do.
- Don't despise your weaknesses; they keep you dependent on God.
- Always remember that it is okay to be different (unique).

> *Don't despise your weaknesses; they keep you dependent on God.*

If we don't have a good relationship with ourselves, we tend to be less authentic. If we don't like ourselves, we often think other people don't like or accept us either, so we pretend to be what we are not, hoping to find acceptance.

If you are angry with yourself, let me ask you: How long have you been that way? Why are you angry with yourself? Perhaps because of your sin, weaknesses, and imperfections? Or is it due to the abilities you lack, the struggles of your past, or not liking the way you look? It is time to make peace with all these issues and make peace with yourself. Remember who you are in Christ. Remember that God Himself created you in your mother's womb (Psalm 139:13–14), and everything He makes is good. Keep in mind what He has done for you by sacrificing His only Son for you. Regardless of what people may think, we all make mistakes, and nobody can do everything right—nobody! That's why the forgiveness that Christ offers is so powerful.

If you can learn to laugh at yourself instead of getting angry, your journey through life will be much more enjoyable. We may be disappointed in ourselves when we sin, but as soon as we repent, God forgives us. We should receive His free gift and do as the apostle Paul taught: Let go of what lies behind and press toward "what is ahead" (Philippians 3:13).

## Do You Like Who You Are?

A lot of people don't like themselves because they don't like the way they look. I always say that if you can do anything to help yourself look better, do it. If not, embrace it and make peace with the parts of yourself that you don't like.

I know a woman who is overweight and finds losing weight very difficult. To lose the extra pounds, she will have to be hungry most of the time, and she isn't willing to do that. She says, "I know I am overweight, but it is my choice to eat what I like." She accepts the fact that if she keeps eating what she likes, she will never be smaller than she currently is. She doesn't dislike herself because of it; she simply realizes it is her choice. She works out regularly, stays healthy, and dresses in styles that complement her. She does what she can to look her best, but she isn't willing to give up the food items that tend to make her "fluffy," as one person put it. She is authentic about her size, she doesn't complain about it or focus on it, and she doesn't make excuses about it. Because she doesn't make a big deal out of it, others tend not to notice it, either.

Don't make excuses when you do things you know you should not do. I was talking recently with a man who has gained forty pounds in the past two years. He commented that he really needs to get back to the gym, and then listed the reasons it is hard for him to do so. We are good friends, and I felt I could be honest with him, so after listening to him for a while, I asked, "You do know you are just making excuses, don't you?" He grinned and said, "My wife told me the same thing."

One of the biggest obstacles to breaking free from things that we don't like about ourselves is making excuses for them. Every time we make an excuse for wrong behavior, it enables us to keep doing it, but if we own our problems and stop making excuses for them, we take the first step toward overcoming them.

> Every time we make an excuse for wrong behavior, it enables us to keep doing it.

We can feel angry at people who can eat anything they want to and are still slim, but that doesn't change the fact that everyone's body does not function the same way. Some people simply have a slower metabolism than others. If that applies to you (and it does apply to me), you can either accept it and adjust accordingly, or you can spend your life with someone you don't like—yourself. Some people are slower than others when trying to accomplish tasks, and no amount of trying to make them hurry will help them move faster. In fact, trying to rush them usually makes the situation worse, not better. That person may have often heard someone complain about how slow they are, and they may see themselves as flawed because of it. They are not flawed; they are simply themselves and should be celebrated, not diminished.

Some people take a long time to make decisions, even about minor issues, and it can irritate those of us who make very fast (sometimes too fast!) decisions. In our irritation, we may be tempted to speak words that can make those people feel bad about themselves. Once again, we need to remember that God has created each of us uniquely, and each of us is amazing in our

*God has created each of us uniquely, and each of us is amazing in our own way.*

own way. Please don't reject or dislike yourself because you are not like someone else. Nothing steals your freedom to be your true self more than comparing yourself with others.

## God Forgives and Forgets

There is a wonderful scripture that makes clear the fact that God wants us to be at peace with ourselves.

> Let him turn away from wickedness and shun it, and let him do right. Let him search for peace (harmony; undisturbedness from fears, agitating passions, and moral conflicts) and seek it eagerly. [Do not merely desire peaceful relations with God, with your fellowmen, and with yourself, but pursue, go after them!]
>
> 1 Peter 3:11 AMPC

If we want peace with ourselves, we must seek it. The word *seek* means "to go after something with intensity." We must pursue and go after peace. This lets us know that peace with anyone is not easy to maintain. The devil wants us divided and angry with everyone, including ourselves. Or, I might even say, *especially* ourselves. If we are angry with ourselves, the anger inside of us will come out of us toward others. It is truly amazing how many of our problems with people are rooted in problems we have with ourselves. If you have difficulty being merciful, you probably don't receive God's mercy. If you

*Many of our problems with people are rooted in problems we have with ourselves.*

have difficulty forgiving others when they make mistakes, you probably treat yourself the same way.

We would all love to be perfect, and although we can have perfect hearts toward God, we will never manifest, or display, perfect behavior as long as we live in a fleshly body. The sooner we accept that, the sooner we will enjoy peace with ourselves. God is not surprised or shocked by our faults, because He knew all of them long before we ever displayed them, and He accepted and loved us in spite of them. God looks at our heart, and the heart is more important to Him than even our behavior. If our heart is right toward God, we will do everything we can to please Him in all of our ways. We will also realize it is not pleasing to Him for us to waste our time and His being angry about something we cannot go back and undo.

Spiritually mature people press past their mistakes and move toward what is ahead of them. Living in the past is useless. The apostle Paul said that it was important for him to forget "what is behind" and to strain "toward what is ahead" (Philippians 3:13). I think most of us spend way too much time dwelling on the past when we should be thinking of and looking to our future.

Our ministry has had the privilege of putting hundreds of thousands of our books into prisons. Perhaps someone in prison is reading this right now, thinking, *What I am reading cannot possibly apply to me after what I have done.* Perhaps they murdered someone or were involved in sex trafficking or other serious crimes. Know this: *If you have repented of your sins, no matter what they were, God has forgiven you and forgotten what you did. He has removed your sin as far as the east is from the west, and He remembers them no more* (Psalm 103:12; Hebrews 8:12). That is amazingly good news, and I urge you to receive it by faith.

No sin is too big for God to forgive. We have all sinned and fallen short of the glory of God (Romans 3:23). And we are all justified by His grace through the redemption that came through Jesus Christ (Romans 3:24). To be justified means to be made just as if you had never sinned. That is an amazing thought to me, one I ponder often. God sees us just as if we had never sinned.

> No sin is too big for God to forgive.

Once a sin is forgiven, washed away by the blood of Jesus, and He remembers it no more, why should we remain angry with ourselves? This is not God's will for us. I think a large majority of people, including Christians, live with the vague fear that God is mad at them or at least that He is not pleased with them. God may not be pleased with certain things we do, but He is always pleased with us as long as we believe in Him.

During Jesus' earthly ministry, some of the people following Him asked, "What must we do to do the works God requires?" Jesus answered, "The work of God is this: to believe in the one he has sent" (John 6:28–29). Our work is to believe in Jesus. Upon hearing that many of us may think, *Yes, and what else?* There is nothing else. We are called believers, and our job is to believe. As part of believing in God, we will see that there are certain things He wants us to do and others He doesn't want us to do, and we will gladly obey. Other than that, we are to believe all of His promises and trust that He will guide us and take care of us.

Jesus told those who were mourning Lazarus's death that if they would only believe, they would "see the glory of God" (John 11:40). If you remember the story, you know that Jesus raised Lazarus from the dead, after he had already been dead four days (John 11:38–44). Jesus taught that believing precedes seeing the glory of God. His glory is the manifestation of all of His excellence. The more we believe, the more of God's power we will experience in our lives.

## Do You Believe?

Do you believe your sins have been forgiven and completely washed away—and that God has totally forgotten them? Do you believe He loves you unconditionally and that nothing can separate you from His love? Do you believe that God is taking care of your problems? The fulfillment of God's promises comes by faith and patience and through continuing to believe while we wait. Faith, patience, and perseverance release peace and joy in our lives. The God of hope fills us with joy and peace as we trust Him (Romans 15:13).

Jesus says, "Whatever you ask for in prayer, believe that you have received it, and it will be yours" (Mark 11:24). He doesn't tell us when we will get it, but if we keep believing, in due time we will receive it. The test of our faith is always found in the waiting. This is like a family waiting in a hospital for the doctor to come out after performing surgery on a beloved family member, hoping

> *The test of our faith is always found in the waiting.*

and praying that the doctor will tell them everything is fine. We are often in God's waiting room, waiting to discover that everything we wanted has arrived and all is well.

For many people, waiting is a time of misery, but it doesn't have to be. If we truly believe that God is faithful and that at the right time He will bring forth the answer to our problem, we can wait peacefully. Just yesterday, God did for me something I had asked Him to do several months ago. Another day this week, God answered a prayer I had prayed only two days before the answer came. Only God can explain why some things take longer than others do. We don't have to understand it; our part is simply to keep believing.

## Are You Receiving What God Is Giving?

I discovered years ago that I was trying to "get" what God had already given me. In actuality, all I needed to do was *receive* it. For example, I would pray for and try to "get" peace without remembering that Jesus gave us His peace (John 14:27). We have peace as a gift from God, but we must choose to walk in it. In the Amplified Bible, Classic Edition version of John 14:27, Jesus says to His followers, "Stop allowing yourselves to be agitated and disturbed," because He had given them His peace.

We don't need to keep praying over and over for the same sin to be forgiven, because God forgives us the first time we ask. However, we need to receive His forgiveness by faith and believe we are forgiven. If we don't, then we still feel guilty and think we should keep asking Him to forgive us.

God's Word says, "Ask and you will receive, and your joy will be complete" (John 16:24). Don't miss what this is saying: Ask *and receive*. Quite often, I start my prayer and fellowship time with God with thanksgiving, and then I take time to sit quietly and receive by faith God's strength, love, peace, joy, healing, and many other wonderful blessings He promises in His Word.

I find the time I spend receiving from God to be very helpful. It reminds me that these gifts are already mine. You might want to try it and see if it helps you also. God's Word includes thousands of promises, and they are for anyone who will believe them. Learn to live in agreement with God. Agree with Him that everything He says about you in His Word is absolutely true, and receive it as freely as it is given.

# PART 2

# Finding the Freedom
# to Be Yourself

# CHAPTER 9

# Don't Let Your Soul Take Control

*For the word of God is alive and active. Sharper than any double-edged sword, it penetrates even to dividing soul and spirit, joints and marrow; it judges the thoughts and attitudes of the heart.*

Hebrews 4:12

When it comes to living authentically and being your unique self, it's important to understand the difference between the soul (the mind, will, and emotions) and the spirit (the inmost part of a person; the heart). I explain them this way: With our spirit, we contact God; with our body, we contact the world; and with our soul, we contact ourselves.

My soul may want to control a situation, yet my spirit may let me know that doing what my soul wants will not please God. In my soul, I may want to do whatever will keep people happy with me, yet my spirit knows that if I do so, I will not be true to myself. We should never go against what we know to be right for us just to keep someone else from being unhappy with us. The only way to live authentically is to learn to follow the Holy Spirit of God, who leads us through our spirit. He does this in many different ways, and a major one is peace. As we do what is right for us, we will have a deep peace about it. If we do what is wrong for us, that sense of peace will be missing. We will feel a discomfort on the inside. It may be ever so slight, yet we just can't get comfortable with what we are thinking about doing.

God's will for us is to learn to be led by His Spirit rather than by our soul. Remember, the soul comprises the mind, the will (our desires and the ability to make choices), and the emotions. I like to say that our mouth gives expression to what is going on in our soul. We speak often about how we feel, what we think, and what we want.

After we are born again, our human spirit is filled with God's Spirit, but our soul is still accustomed to being in control. As we grow in spiritual maturity, submitting to the will of God, the soul *gradually* comes under the control of the Holy Spirit. This happens little by little as we learn God's will through His Word and we no longer allow our soul to be in control. We might say that we surrender our self-will a little at a time.

When I began my journey with God, I was born again, but I was a carnal (fleshly) Christian. In other words, I lived my life according to the flesh (body and soul), not according to the Spirit. Initially, if I didn't get my way, I responded with anger and self-pity. My soul was in control. Through the years, God changed me, and although I am not yet perfect by any means, I have learned that I can control my soul and not allow it to run my life. I may feel like getting angry or feeling sorry for myself at times, but that doesn't mean I have to do so. We are daily faced with many situations in which we must decide if we will follow the soul or the Spirit.

According to the apostle Paul, people who walk in the Spirit will not fulfill the lusts (desires) of the flesh (Galatians 5:16). Our goal as children of God should be to always follow the guidance of the Holy Spirit, no matter what we think, how we feel, or what we want. The more we love Jesus, the more we want to obey Him and walk according to the Spirit. Jesus says, "If you love me, keep my commands" (John 14:15). I have found that my love for Jesus has grown over time, and the more I love Him, the more I want to please Him. Our love for Jesus grows as we observe and experience His goodness, love, mercy, forgiveness, kindness, and many other wonderful attributes.

> I refuse to be angry and waste my days in self-pity because I have not gotten my way about something.

I refuse to be angry and waste my days in self-pity because I have not gotten my way about something. I have learned that if I don't get what I want, God must have something better in mind. I trust Him, and that allows me to be at peace. However, it has taken forty-five years for me to get from where I started to where I am today. Maybe you will be a faster learner than I was, but I had a soul full of wounds, bruises, and pain from childhood abuse, rejection, and abandonment. David writes in Psalm 23:3 (NKJV) that the Lord restores our soul. Isaiah the prophet writes that He gives us "beauty for ashes, the oil of joy for mourning, the garment of praise for the spirit of heaviness" (Isaiah 61:3 NKJV). Isaiah also writes that because He is a God of justice, He will give us a double recompense (reward) for our former trouble (Isaiah 61:7 AMPC).

Having a soul that is whole—not broken, wounded, or full of pain—is vital to being able to stop people-pleasing behavior or any other bad behavior. As I learned to live out of my authentic self and stop using so much energy trying to please people, I had to understand what the soul was and realize that I did not have to let my mind, will, and emotions control me. One of the most important and empowering lessons I have learned in my walk with God is that I do not have to let my soul be in charge, and that I can control it.

We can choose our own thoughts instead of just accepting and meditating on whatever pops into our head. We can feel something, yet live beyond how we feel. And we can want to do something but resist the desire to do it if we know it is not God's will for us. We need God's help in all of this, because apart from Him we can do nothing (John 15:5). He is our strength, but He allows us to make our decisions. God has no desire to control us. He has given each of us a free will, and He wants us to use our will to choose to follow His will, not ours, for our lives.

In order to follow God's will, we must be educated in God's Word so we know what His will is. The scripture at the beginning of this chapter tells us that the Word of God will divide soul and spirit. In other words, it shows us what is right and wrong, true and false.

If my mind keeps telling me I am no good and people don't like me, but God's Word tells me that God made me, that what He creates is good, and that He will give me favor with people, then I can choose to think and meditate on what God says. I can refuse the random thoughts that will wander in and out of my mind incessantly if I let them.

## Fight for Your Freedom

As long as we allow the soul to be in control, we are not free. We must "fight the good fight of faith" (1 Timothy 6:12 KJV) and stand firm on God's Word, believing it above all else. Paul writes in Romans 12:2 that we are not to be conformed to this world, "but be transformed by the renewing of your mind." To renew the mind means to learn to think differently than the world thinks and to learn to think as God does. We renew our mind by studying God's Word.

Remembering that your mind is part of your soul, take a look at this scripture:

The weapons we fight with are not the weapons of the world. On the contrary, they have divine power to demolish strongholds. We demolish arguments and every pretension that sets itself up against the knowledge of God, and we take captive every thought to make it obedient to Christ.

2 Corinthians 10:4–5

The Amplified Bible, Classic Edition translation of 2 Corinthians 10:5 says it this way: "[We] refute arguments and theories and reasonings and every proud and lofty thing that sets itself up against the [true] knowledge of God." These are all processes of the mind. It continues in verse 5 to say that we are to bring our thoughts captive to Christ: "We lead every thought and purpose away captive into the obedience of Christ." This means we can say no to wrong thoughts and replace them with right ones. We may do the same with emotions (feelings). The fact that I may feel angry doesn't mean that I have to behave angrily. I can behave in a godly way, no matter how I feel.

> We can say no to wrong thoughts and replace them with right ones.

As we fight this good fight of faith, the apostle Paul encourages us not to "grow weary and lose heart" (Hebrews 12:3) and not to "become weary in doing good" (Galatians 6:9). This means we are not to become weary of doing the right thing, "for at the proper time we will reap a harvest if we do not give up" (Galatians 6:9). Doing the right thing does not necessarily mean that we will get right results immediately. At times our faith is tested, and we must stand firm, continuing to do the right thing regardless of how we feel. If we do, we are promised a harvest in due time.

When someone asks you to do something you do not have peace about doing, and you know you should say no to it, your mind may be screaming, *If I say no, they won't like me anymore. They will think I am selfish.* Your emotions may push you to do what you know you should not do simply to keep the peace with the one making the request. If you give in and do what you *feel* like doing, unfortunately you are feeding your soul and keeping it strong, but if you stand firm (with God's help) and do what you know you should do, regardless of how you feel, you will weaken the power your soul has over you. Each time you confront a similar situation and respond properly to it, your soul will lose a little more control.

When considering the soul, we should realize that our free will is the big boss. No matter what we think or how we feel, we can choose to follow either the soul or the Holy Spirit. God will always help us follow Him if that is what we choose.

> When considering the soul, we should realize that our free will is the big boss.

## The Root of the Problem

Your struggles with people-pleasing may not be rooted in the same experiences as mine, but all problems have a root—a situation that triggered the fearful or wrong behavior. I developed the habit of people-pleasing because of my tormenting fear of my father. He became angry if I didn't do everything exactly as he wanted me to do it, and his anger terrified me. Because of my extreme fear, I fell into the bad habit of simply doing whatever would keep everyone happy, especially if they had a very strong personality or tended to show anger or displeasure when they didn't get what they wanted.

I'm sure there were many other rootlets of the problem of people-pleasing, such as being afraid people wouldn't like me if

I didn't keep them happy all the time. But that fear was based on the fact that I didn't like myself, so I assumed no one else would like me, either. I continually felt that I had to earn everyone's acceptance, so you can imagine what a relief it was to me to learn that Father God accepted me simply because I believed in Jesus and trusted Him as my Savior and that I didn't need to perform in any certain way to get Him to love me.

Freedom didn't truly come until I realized that not everyone would like me and I was okay with that. I trusted God to give me the friends that were right for me. You can survive rejection, believe it or not. Not everyone has to think you are wonderful for you to have a great life. I have heard that 10 percent of all people won't like us no matter who we are or what we do, so why would we focus on the few who don't, when 90 percent do?

Although I was a people-pleaser in some of my relationships, I was a controller in others. I came under the power of those with a strong personality, especially those who reminded me of my father, but I controlled those who were mild-mannered or more easygoing than I was, if they would let me. I found it interesting that I didn't respect those who allowed me to control them and actually wished they would confront me, so those people I let control me must have felt the same way.

## The Problem with Willpower

Although we have a free will, we cannot use willpower alone to overcome our weaknesses without help from God. It is a big mistake to think we can overcome something like people-pleasing simply by trying. First, we need revelation (realization) that we have a problem, and second, we must talk to God about the problem and ask Him to set us free. In this way, we do make an effort, but it is an effort made in the Spirit, not the flesh, and we do only what the Holy Spirit leads us to do, not what our friends have done, or what we *think* may work.

Consider this passage from *The Life that Wins*, by Watchman Nee, a Chinese church leader and Christian teacher and author imprisoned for his faith from 1952 until his death in 1972:

> The first step to take is to tell Him, "O God, I cannot, and I will not. I am finished, I give up trying, I will fight no more." This is yielding. This marks the first step towards deliverance. Formerly, I thought I could change my pride somewhat; now, Lord I will not try again. Formerly, I reasoned I could improve my temper a little; now, Lord, I quit altogether. Formerly I imagined I could somehow control my tongue; now, Lord, I give up. I cannot, I will not try to change, I give up completely."

This is called yielding, meaning to submit ourselves to God's leading. We must yield completely to Jesus, letting Him know that we believe we can do nothing apart from Him. For example, I remember a time when all God had me do was confess specific promises from His Word over my life three times each day. I continued this for six months and started seeing changes in myself. At other times, He has led me to certain books that have really helped me. On several occasions, He led me to fast for a set period of time. In addition, He always uses His Word to renew our minds so we can think as He does. Yielding to God doesn't mean we do nothing, but it does mean that we do nothing unless we truly believe God is leading us to do it.

The Book of Romans gives us good insight on yielding to God and not to our flesh.

> Let not sin therefore rule as king in your mortal (short-lived, perishable) bodies, to make you yield to its cravings and be subject to its lusts and evil passions. Do not continue offering or yielding your bodily members [and faculties] to sin as instruments (tools) of wickedness. But offer and yield yourselves to God as though you have been raised from the dead to [perpetual] life, and your bodily members [and faculties] to God, presenting them as implements of righteousness.
>
> Romans 6:12–13 AMPC

We yield and God does what we cannot do. "What is impossible with man is possible with God" (Luke 18:27).

When I began studying God's Word seriously, I quickly realized I had a lot of problems in my behavior, so I set out to change myself using my willpower. Had my plan worked, I would have taken credit for its success and used it to justify telling other people to do what I did.

My plan didn't work because God had to allow me to come to the end of my own self-effort and yield myself completely to Him. It was at this juncture in my life that I found out about His grace. I knew I was *saved* by grace, but I wasn't *living* by grace. I had received salvation without any effort on my part, but somehow, I thought I had to change myself through my own strength. One day, I saw a scripture that was life-changing for me:

> Are you so foolish and so senseless and so silly? Having begun [your new life spiritually] with the [Holy] Spirit, are you now reaching perfection [by dependence] on the flesh?
>
> Galatians 3:3 AMPC

My eyes were opened, and I learned that just as I was saved by grace, I would be changed by grace. Grace is God's favor coming to us freely even though we don't deserve it. But grace is also God's power coming to us to enable us to do with ease what we could never do on our own with any amount of struggle or effort.

When I felt convicted of ungodly behavior, I learned to admit it, to ask God to change me, and to be willing to change. If He wanted me to make a certain decision or take a certain action, I asked Him to show me what it was. I no longer tried on my own to do what only God could do, and I did begin to change over the years. I give God all the credit for what He has done in my life. I still have many changes to look forward to, but I can enjoy where I am on the way to where I am going, and you can also. Yes, you can accept and enjoy yourself even while you are still imperfect. You can have a perfect heart toward God and still display imperfect behavior. There is a big difference between wickedness and weakness. Everyone has weaknesses, but that doesn't mean we are wicked or ungodly.

> You can accept and enjoy yourself even while you are still imperfect.

When we let our soul try to change itself, we are still putting the soul in control, and that is not what we want to do. When the temptation to please people instead of God comes to us, we are to resist it in the strength of God, and not by willpower alone. Let Him fill your will with His strength, flood your mind with His thoughts, and give you His desires to replace wild emotion. Then and only then can you have a soul *under* control instead of a soul that is *in* control.

# CHAPTER 10

# The Need for Approval

*A man cannot be comfortable without his own approval.*

Mark Twain

We should never sacrifice our authenticity to gain the approval of other people. We should believe that God approves of us, and we should approve of ourselves. In order to do that, we must learn how to separate what we do from who we are. As I've said for years, we need to separate our *who* from our *do*. This is vital to living a life of authenticity and to a strong, growing relationship with God.

> *We must learn how to separate what we do from who we are.*

As a believer in Jesus Christ, you are a child of God. Just as God told Jeremiah that He approved of him as His chosen instrument before he was formed in his mother's womb (Jeremiah 1:5 AMPC), so He approves of you. He doesn't approve of everything you do, but He does approve of you if you believe in Jesus as your Lord and Savior.

I don't approve of everything my children or grandchildren do, but I approve of them as my family. We may have disagreements about some issues or situations, but we are—and always will be—family. You are part of God's family. He is your Father, Jesus is your Savior and Lord, and the Holy Spirit is your Comforter, Guide, Teacher, Advocate, Intercessor, and Helper. You are part of the best family that exists. In addition, to that you are part of God's kingdom family, which consists of all believers everywhere.

In order to approve of yourself, you must make decisions you believe are right for you rather than going against your heart in order to please people who want you to do something you don't have peace about doing. The more we need the approval of other people, the more likely we are to live an unhappy and dissatisfied life. Are you giving up your own happiness in an effort to keep others happy and pleased with you? If you are, I urge you to find the courage to say no to people when you feel you need to do so.

> *The more we need the approval of other people, the more likely we are to live an unhappy and dissatisfied life.*

When Dave and I shop together for clothes for me, he often wants me to buy something that he likes on me but that I don't like. Just to gain his approval, I used to purchase those items to please him, but I ended up never wearing them. He wasn't trying to control me, but I let the fear of his disapproval control me. Interestingly, I began to notice that when I liked something on him and he didn't like it, he refused to buy it. Now if I don't like something he wants me to wear, I respectfully say, "No, I don't like how it looks on me." Even if he tries to talk me into it, I hold firm. We can never be ourselves until we let the fear of disapproval stop controlling our decisions.

Maybe this Saturday you plan to finish several projects you have been putting off for a long time. Then a friend calls and asks if you can babysit her three children so she and her husband can take a short weekend trip. Your heart sinks when you hear the request, because this particular friend usually expresses her disapproval when she doesn't get her way. Will you forget your plans and say yes simply to please her? Or will you be bold and say, "I'm sorry, but I can't because I already have other plans"?

She will probably ask what the plans are, and getting your projects done won't seem important to her. That is the point at which you will need to stand your ground, remembering that your projects may not be important to her, but they are significant to you. She may even express her disapproval of your choice, or she may become angry with you or give you the cold shoulder for a while,

> If you always say yes to everyone who asks something of you, then your life will not be your life.

but going through her negative emotions while not bowing to her demands is the only way for you to establish boundaries and break free from letting other people's desires control you.

At times you may feel that God wants you to change your plans and do something for a friend, but if you always say yes to everyone who asks something of you, then your life will not be *your* life. When people truly love and care for you, they will not become angry if you tell them you are unable to do what they ask you to do. A true friend wants you to follow your heart and God's guidance.

It is impossible to please all of the people all of the time. If you learn that lesson early in life and decide to do only what you have peace about doing, you will save yourself a lot of trouble and heartache. A major way that God speaks to us and guides us is by the presence or absence of peace. When peace is present, it is a yes from God, and when it is absent, it is a no from Him. The

> It is impossible to please all of the people all of the time.

Bible says that we should let peace be the "umpire" in our life, "deciding and settling with finality all questions that arise" in our minds (Colossians 3:15 AMPC).

God's Word does say that we are to please people and not live only to please ourselves (Romans 15:1–2), but that doesn't mean we should please people if doing what they want us to do goes against God's will or what we sincerely feel in our heart we should do. Sometimes we have to wait awhile before we can determine whether we have peace about an action or not. In that case, then we should not act prematurely. There is no harm in telling someone who wants you to do something that you want to think about it or pray about it.

## Addicted to Approval

An addiction is something that controls people—something they feel they cannot do without or something they do to alleviate pain or pressure. It comes in many forms. People can be addicted to drugs, alcohol, gambling, sex, shopping, eating, work—and yes, even approval. Like all addicts, insecure people look for a "fix" when they get unhappy. They need someone to reaffirm them and assure them that everything is all right. Being in relationship with someone who is extremely insecure can be very exhausting because of how needy they are. We have compassion for these people and want to help them, but getting an approval fix each time they feel insecure will not set them free. They need to find their confidence and security in God. I know this, because I was once this way, and it exhausted my husband. He felt that no matter what he did, I was never happy.

The good news is that people who are addicted to approval don't have to suffer with insecurity; there is a cure for approval addiction. The Word of God says we can be secure through Jesus Christ, "rooted and established in [His] love" (Ephesians 3:17). This means we are free to be ourselves and become all we can be in Him.

I wasted many years of my life addicted to approval. It began during my early childhood years in my relationship with my father. He was an angry man who never seemed to approve of anyone or anything, but I was so afraid of his anger that I tried to always do what I thought would meet with his approval somehow.

My fear of him only grew as he began to abuse me sexually, not only forcing me to do things that I hated, but also forcing me to keep them a secret. My mother always tried to please him too, because she was also afraid of him. No one confronted him about anything. I don't ever remember feeling relaxed and safe around my father.

Of course, I carried the emotional habits of people-pleasing and seeking approval into my adult life. Anytime I thought the important people in my life didn't approve of what I was doing, saying, wearing, or planning, I quickly changed so they would think well of me. I craved approval above all else, just as drug addicts crave their drugs.

If I met with disapproval, I was totally miserable, anxious, and worried until I was sure I had fixed the situation. I will forever be thankful that God taught me that my job was to please Him and that in doing so, I would be pleased. There are many times when God does lead me to do what another person wants me to do, even though I might not be thrilled about it. But when I know I am pleasing God in doing it, I can do it with joy. We are not to be selfish and should try to please people in healthy, balanced ways but not be so addicted to pleasing others that we disobey God in the process.

I'm sure you know what I am talking about. Even if you are not an approval addict, my guess is that if you get a new haircut that is a little out of the norm for you, you don't feel quite comfortable about it until someone compliments you or gives you a nod of approval.

If you wear a new dress and ask a friend how she likes it, what do you do if she says, "I think it makes you look a little larger than you really are"? Do you never wear it again, or do you go ahead and wear it because you like it? I admit that when that happens to me, sometimes I have to force myself to keep wearing something because I refuse to give in to the approval addiction from which God has set me free. If ten people expressed the same opinion about it, I probably wouldn't wear it again, but the opinion of one person is just that—one person's opinion, which isn't any better than yours is.

Different people like different styles, and they should be free to enjoy wearing the style they like and feel comfortable in, except when they need to follow a particular dress code for a job or a special occasion. I rarely wear jeans because I am not comfortable in them. I prefer softer material. However, a lot of people try to get me to wear jeans more often, telling me how good they look on me, that they are in style, that everyone wears them, and so on. But I don't want to wear them, so I usually don't. If I find a pair that is really comfortable, I will wear them occasionally, but even then, they just are not my go-to pants. It is interesting how often people try to get you to like what they like and cannot understand why you don't. The reason is that you are a unique individual and are free to follow your desires without apologizing for them.

## Insecurity

Our society today suffers from an epidemic of insecurity. Many people are insecure, which can and often does lead to a constant need for an approval fix. For example, if a wife cooks dinner and everyone in the family doesn't compliment her, then she may be convinced that no one liked it and will be miserable the rest of the evening. We all need and enjoy encouragement and compliments, but if we cannot be happy unless people give them, then our need for such affirmation is out of balance and our enemy, Satan, can use it against us. The one who prepared the meal should simply ask if everyone liked dinner, but if she is afraid of rejection, she won't. She will just go on imagining that no one enjoyed it when there is a good chance they did enjoy it but simply did not comment on it.

Someone came to me many years ago and told me that a woman who attended one of my Bible studies was hurt because I didn't speak to her when I passed her in the hallway. The truth was that I didn't even see her. It was not my desire to hurt her or anyone else, but I quickly discovered that insecure people crave attention from those they see as important. Since I taught the Bible study, she viewed me as important. Therefore, attention from me would have made her feel important. God doesn't want us to get our security in that way. He wants us to be secure in His love for us. He may have actually prevented me from seeing her because He wanted her to learn that she was very important whether I spoke to her or not.

People who have been hurt through rejection or abandonment often seek others' approval to alleviate the pain of low self-esteem. This may work for a while, but eventually the continual need for approval becomes a burden not only to the person who needs it but also to those who are pressured to give it.

A woman with low self-esteem may give her husband the job of keeping her feeling good about herself through a daily fix of compliments. If he doesn't give them, she may feel bad about herself all day. The best plan is to trust God for the encouragement you need and let Him give it to you through whomever He chooses to use, or to give it to you Himself.

As we grow spiritually, we should be more concerned about encouraging others than we are about their encouraging us. Spiritual growth means growing in your knowledge of who you are in Christ and receiving your worth and value from Him and His love. The more convinced you are that God loves you, the less you will need other people to tell you that you are acceptable.

> *As we grow spiritually, we should be more concerned about encouraging others than we are about their encouraging us.*

We are made acceptable to God through our faith (Romans 5:1). It is not our pretty outfit, our level of education, who we know, or how naturally talented we are that makes us acceptable to God. We are acceptable to Him through faith and faith alone. People may think more highly of us if we have those other things, but God doesn't, and He is the one who really matters.

## The Foundation for Security

Every building must have a strong foundation to stand on, or it will crumble in storms or high winds. You and I also need a strong foundation in order to fulfill our destiny and live a blessed and joy-filled life. We need the foundation of knowing and being secure in the fact that we are loved unconditionally and more than we could ever ask for or imagine. We cannot be assured of getting that kind of security from people, but we can have it through a relationship with God. His will is for each of us to be secure so we will not be tormented or hindered in life because of a lack of confidence. I believe the foundation for security and confidence is accepting God's unconditional love and abiding in it each day, while also accepting ourselves even though we realize we have weaknesses and are not perfect.

Jesus took our sin and gave us His righteousness (Romans 5:21; 2 Corinthians 5:21). Or, to look at it another way, Jesus took our wrongness and gave us His rightness. We no longer have to obsessively think about what is wrong with us, but we can realize we are made right with God through faith in Christ. I know I have faults, but I don't think about them very often unless God is dealing with me about a particular fault in order to bring healthy change to my life.

When we receive Christ, old things (our old condition) pass away, and all things are made new in Him (2 Corinthians 5:17). We become new spiritual clay, so to speak. God is the potter, and we should relax and let Him work in us as He sees fit. Let me encourage you to be the kind of clay that is pliable and moldable in the potter's hand, not the hard, crumbly kind that is difficult to shape. Learn God's ways and easily adapt to them rather than stubbornly resisting and rebelling against change.

If clay had feelings, I don't imagine it would understand or enjoy the molding process, but it would like the end result of being transformed from a lump of gray clay into a beautiful cup, vase, or bowl. I encourage you to be secure enough to trust God's process in your life. Even if you don't understand exactly what God is making of you, remember that He loves you and that everything He does is good.

# CHAPTER 11

# Freedom from Comparison

*Comparison is the death of joy.*

Mark Twain

Let me encourage you to enjoy being the person you are without comparing yourself to anyone else and trying to do what they do or trying to be someone you were never meant to be. You are

> *You are valuable to God for who you are, not for what you do.*

valuable to God for *who you are*, not for *what you do*. Do what you do for Him, but don't ever think your value to Him is based on it. One person may be the CEO of the company and

another the janitor, but both are equally valuable to God, and both should use their talents to serve God and be joyful in doing so.

God called me to be the teacher in our ministry and He called Dave to carry out other responsibilities that are equally important but not as visible as my role. People frequently ask Dave if my being the one in front of the audience instead of him has been hard for him. It only took him about three weeks to learn that as long as he did what God was asking him to do, he would have the grace to do it with ease, and it would give him joy. But if he tried to be something he was not, then he would be frustrated and have no joy.

I can say without hesitation that Dave is one of the happiest, most secure, most peaceful people I know, and we both believe this is partially because he is doing what God has asked him to do without comparing himself to anyone else.

We all have strengths and weaknesses, and the devil likes to remind us of what we are not able to do. He tempts us to compare ourselves with others who have talents that we don't have, but we should steadfastly resist that temptation. No one of us can manufacture a talent that God did not give us.

> The devil likes to remind us of what we are not able to do.

A former pastor of ours once told Dave he should be doing the teaching in our home Bible study, not me. Dave tried to teach, and I tried to be quiet—and it didn't work. It is amazing how miserable we make ourselves trying to do what others think we should be doing. What God had called me to do was certainly not the norm in those days, but He wanted to do something unique. We simply needed to obey. And guess what? It worked! Forty-five years later we are still doing what God called us to do, and many people have come into God's kingdom and been helped by His grace and mercy.

In John 3, an argument arose between some of John's disciples and a certain Jew about the matter of ceremonial washing. They said to John, "Rabbi, that man who was with you on the other side of the Jordan—the one you testified about—look, he is baptizing, and everyone is going to him" (John 3:25–26). John's disciples were comparing the size of the crowd the other man was drawing to the size of John's crowds. The other man's crowds were bigger, and it was obviously making them feel insecure, but John told them, "A person can receive only what is given them from heaven" (John 3:27). John went on to remind them that he was not the Messiah but had been sent ahead of the Messiah to prepare His way. John found joy in doing the part God had given him to do and said it was time for Jesus to increase but for him to decrease (John 3:28–30). John was secure and had no need to compete with or compare himself to Jesus. It is wonderful when we are secure enough not to compete, compare, or be jealous of anyone.

As children, we begin comparing ourselves with other people, and doing so is not a problem if we simply realize that everyone is different and we have a solid understanding of our personal worth and value. However, if we don't, then every minute we spend comparing ourselves to someone else is a minute wasted from our own lives, because no matter how hard we try, we cannot be someone else. Other people we admire may be examples for us, but they should not become our ideal, nor should being like them become our goal in life.

God delights in reminding us that He created us and that each of us is unique and valuable. We are one of a kind. Insecurity comes from looking at our flaws, weaknesses, sins, and inabilities without also looking at our strengths and abilities and remembering that our goal is to be like Jesus and no one else. Freedom from insecurity comes from looking to Jesus, the "pioneer and perfecter" of our faith (Hebrews 12:2). If we look away from all else and look to Jesus, then before long insecurity will be a distant memory, and a brand-new, secure self will be enjoying life.

We are unique, which means we are not and never were meant to be like someone else. God loves infinite variety. If you don't believe that, just take a day and watch nature videos or programs about animals and see how many varieties there are on every continent. There are between ten thousand and thirteen thousand species of birds. Ants are tiny and we rarely even think of them, but there are more than ten thousand known species of ants around the world. And there are more than forty-five thousand species of spiders on earth, and scientists have named one million species of insects, with perhaps as many as four million still uncategorized. Yes, God loves variety!

I love watching nature shows because they remind me of the immensity and creativity of God and of how awesome He is. Just think of all the different kinds of trees and flowers. When I walk down my street, what makes the scenery so beautiful is that everything is not just alike. There are many kinds of trees, bushes, and flowers. Although they are all different, they blend together perfectly, making something amazing to see and enjoy. We should celebrate our differences rather than wishing we were like someone else. Think how boring and bland the world would be if everyone and everything were just alike.

Perhaps we insult God's creativity when we try to be like someone else, since He has gone to such lengths to make us all different. In my prideful youth, I thought everyone should be like me, and since they were not, I stayed busy trying to change them. After we started Joyce Meyer Ministries and it grew to the point where we had about fifty employees, I was frustrated all the time because I kept trying to get people to complete tasks they were not gifted to do, but I didn't realize it at the time. I critically thought, *What is wrong with you?!* I'm sure that my incessant dissatisfaction with people made them feel they were unacceptable and maybe even as though they had failed.

Dave and I are very different, and for years we had a lot of arguments that were caused by my trying to make him be like me. I treated my children the same way. But God was gracious to me, to my family, and to our employees, and He put a book into my hands titled *The Spirit-Controlled Temperament*, written by Tim LaHaye and published by Tyndale Momentum. I learned from

that book that people are divided into several groups of temperaments. Within those God-given temperaments, we have a variety
of sub-traits that make us all uniquely different.

There are many books along these lines, and they all have their
own unique way of describing the different types of people that
exist. Tim LaHaye's book categorizes the temperaments into four
groups: sanguine, choleric, melancholy, and phlegmatic. I am
choleric, and Dave is phlegmatic. These are two opposite temperaments, and like Dave and me, most people are drawn to someone
whose personality is the opposite of theirs. Not only do people
have a primary temperament, but most also have a secondary
temperament. For example, one of my sons is half choleric and
half sanguine. The other son is 99.9 percent choleric. They both
accomplish a lot because of their choleric temperament, but the
one with the sanguine subtemperament also has to have lots of
fun, so he handles his schedule differently than his brother does.
One son is scheduled and methodical, while the other is more
likely to do business on the phone while flying down a mountain
on a snowboard. They both do a good job, but they have two very
different ways of doing it. Both ways work. An important truth
we need to realize if we ever want to truly be ourselves is that different is not bad. This is also the only way we can get along with
other people and enjoy healthy relationships with them.

## The Four Temperaments

I want to give a brief description of each type of temperament
here, but if you want to study the temperaments more deeply, I
recommend that you read some good books available on the subject. I like *Spirit-Controlled Temperament* because it is easy to read
and simple to understand.

## Sanguine

Tim LaHaye writes that sanguines have a "warm, buoyant, lively, and fun-loving temperament." They are led by feelings rather than reason, and feelings dominate many of their decisions. Sanguines make friends easily, feel empathetic toward those who are hurting, and have the gift of making the people they meet feel important. They have no trouble enjoying themselves immensely and can pass on their enjoyment to others. In fact, sanguine people are motivated by fun and enjoyment. This teaches us that someone who is half choleric and half sanguine will accomplish a great deal and have a lot of fun doing it.

## Choleric

LaHaye says that cholerics are "often self-sufficient and very independent" and that they tend "to be decisive and opinionated, finding it easy to make decisions" not only for themselves, but also others. A choleric "thrives on activity" and is characterized by stubbornness and determination. They do not need their environment to activate them but activate their environment. "He is not frightened by adversities: in fact, they tend to encourage him."

In other books, I have read that the choleric is motivated by accomplishment. I am a choleric, and I can verify each of these qualities. If I can accomplish something each day, then I am a satisfied person.

## Melancholy

Melancholy is usually considered to be "the 'dark' temperament," and it is characterized by sensitivity and the capacity for deep feelings. LaHaye writes: "Actually, he is the richest of all the temperaments." He goes on to explain that melancholies are "analytical, self-sacrificing, gifted," and they tend to be perfectionists. People with the melancholy temperament are usually introverts, but their moods often dominate them, so they behave according to how they feel. Sometimes they are ecstatic, and at other times they are depressed. They are faithful friends and said to have the most dependable of all the temperaments.

I have noticed that melancholies are also motivated by order. They love lists and plans and don't do well when life is disorganized.

## Phlegmatic

LaHaye refers to the phlegmatic person as "Flip Phlegmatic." People with this personality type have a "calm, cool, slow, easy going, well-balanced temperament." They are not easily bothered or flustered, regardless of the circumstance. They rarely erupt in anger or burst out in laughter, but their emotions stay steady, level, and under control. They are consistent and kindhearted, but rarely show their true feelings. LaHaye notes, "Phlegmatics do not lack for friends because they enjoy people and have a naturally dry sense of humor that others enjoy." In my experience, phlegmatics are motivated by peace. As long as they can have peace, they are happy.

These descriptions are very brief, and I do encourage you to read more on the subject of temperaments, because understanding them will help you learn a lot about yourself and the people with whom you are in relationship. Once you see that we are all unique and born with different temperaments, you can easily understand why comparing yourself with other people is a waste of time.

Studying this subject helped me immensely as I learned how to accept and get along with people. I realized that everyone could not be like I am simply because I wanted them to. God has created each of us to be different, and when we work together, one person's strengths compensate for others' weaknesses. Learning to accept people and help them feel valuable is one of the best gifts we can give them. As I have heard and repeated many times, people don't always remember what we said to them, but they do remember how we made them feel.

> Learning to accept people and help them feel valuable is one of the best gifts we can give them.

When we are free from comparing ourselves with other people or comparing them with ourselves, life becomes much easier, more peaceful, and more joy filled. This also puts a smile on God's face because He delights in our individuality and uniqueness.

## The Peacock and the Crow

I came across a short story that illustrates how futile comparison is, and I want to share it with you.

A crow lived in the forest and was absolutely satisfied in life. But one day he saw a swan. *This swan is so white*, he thought, *and I am so black. This swan must be the happiest bird in the world.*

He expressed his thoughts to the swan. "Actually," the swan replied, "I was feeling that I was the happiest bird around until I saw a parrot, which has two colors. I now think the parrot is the happiest bird in creation." The crow then approached the parrot. The parrot explained, "I lived a very happy life until I saw a peacock. I have only two colors, but the peacock has multiple colors."

The crow then visited a peacock in the zoo and saw that hundreds of people had gathered to see him. After the people had left, the crow approached the peacock. "Dear peacock," the crow said, "you are so beautiful. Everyday thousands of people come to see you. When people see me, they immediately shoo me away. I think you are the happiest bird on the planet."

The peacock replied, "I always thought that I was the most beautiful and happy bird on the planet. But because of my beauty, I am entrapped in this zoo. I have examined the zoo very carefully, and I have realized that the crow is the only bird not kept in a cage. So for the past few days I have been thinking that if I were a crow, I could happily roam everywhere."

That's our problem too. We make unnecessary comparison with others and become sad. We don't value what God has given us. This leads to the vicious cycle of unhappiness. Learn to be happy in what you have instead of looking at what you don't have. There will always be someone who will have more or less than you have. People who are satisfied with who they are and what they have are the happiest people in the world.

As the crow discovered, everyone has strengths and weaknesses. Some people have opportunities and strengths others do not have, but those people have different opportunities and different strengths. At the same time, everyone also has weak-nesses and limitations, which is why we need each other and why healthy relationships are so important.

Let me encourage you today to recognize, appreciate, and value all the positive aspects of who you are and everything that is good about other people. Don't compare yourself with them; celebrate them and celebrate your authentic, unique self.

# CHAPTER 12

# Are You Stuck in the Control Trap?

*True love is built on free will and free choice, not control and manipulation.*

Ken Poirot

If you have ever encountered a controlling person, you know that being under their influence is like being trapped. Although they didn't ensnare you physically, their control impacted your thinking so negatively that you may have felt trapped, unable to express your true feelings or to do what you wanted to do. Maybe you are living in that situation right now. If you have ever been controlled or are being controlled currently, this chapter will help you understand how control operates. The better you understand it, the sooner you can begin to break free from it.

We often ask why the people who try to control us behave as they do, but we should ask instead why we allow them to do it. I once worked for someone who had a very controlling personality. I really liked and needed my job, so I often cowered under his unreasonable demands because I was afraid of being fired if I stood up to him. When I finally did find the courage to follow my heart and leave, I found myself angry with the employer who had controlled me for several years. Then I got a surprise when

God told me that I was just as guilty as he was, because I *let* him control me.

Yes, if you are being controlled you have a responsibility to stop it. As long as you allow it to go on, you enable abusive behavior.

Breaking free from control requires confrontation, which is something that many people find very hard to do. Why? Because we know that confrontation usually brings anger and blame, so we just keep doing the same old thing and hating it. We even disrespect ourselves for allowing it to go on, yet we do nothing to stop it.

I have been both a controller and a person who has been controlled, so I know and understand both sides of the control equation. People control others and allow themselves to be controlled mainly out of fear, but someone who controls others is also selfish and usually has an exaggerated opinion of their own importance. In their pride, they are convinced that their way is the only right way to do things, and they insist they be done that way. They are rarely open to listening to other opinions, let alone actually considering them valuable.

## Control Creates Fear

Let's look at people who try to control others. Normally, they not only try to control people, but they also try to be in charge of what happens around them—their circumstances and their environment. They have a desire or a plan, and they expect others to give up their lives and help them get what they want.

One of the primary ways people try to control others is by instilling fear in them. Because my father was a controller, he managed to create fear in everyone in the family—my mother, my brother, and me. My mother was fearful of him and never really had a life of her own. For that matter, she didn't have much of a life at all. She wasn't allowed to go to church or to have any personal friends my father didn't approve of, and she was verbally and physically abused.

She was given a small allowance each week and often had to account for the ways she used it. She cooked what my father wanted to eat, when he wanted to eat it. He worked the three p.m. to midnight shift as a truck mechanic and often wanted to eat when he returned home after midnight, so my mother dutifully got out of bed and prepared his food. Her job required her to be at work early in the morning, but he never considered that interrupting her sleep was selfish and left her tired the next day.

My mother was what we would call today a battered woman. My father often slapped her in the face, hit her, and even beat her a few times. He drank alcohol heavily on the weekends, and although he was generally mean, he grew meaner when he was drunk. I was repulsed by my mother's lack of initiative. Even though she knew my father would surely be with another woman when he went drinking, she laid out his best clothes and made sure his shirt was flawlessly ironed for his nights out.

I loved my mother, but I hated her weakness. Her timidity made me disrespect her. Not only did she suffer, but her failure to confront my father permitted my brother and me to suffer also. Fear is a formidable enemy, and when people are in its grip, they act in ways that do not reflect what is truly in their hearts. I know my mother wished she had the courage to leave my father or at the very least confront him, but fear kept her frozen in place.

Even though my mother was aware that my father was sexually abusing me on a regular basis, she did nothing about it. That is still a mystery to me. I cannot imagine any mother letting her husband sexually abuse her children and doing nothing, but great fear can make people so timid and cowardly that they are unable to do anything but survive.

My brother joined the Marines at seventeen years old in order to get away from home. As soon as I turned eighteen years old, I moved out of the house one night while my father was at work. Even though I got away from the problem, I took the problem with me in my soul. I lived another twenty years in my own dysfunctional behavior before I began allowing God to heal me. Thank God, He did heal me, but that journey of healing and wholeness took many years of Bible study, application of God's Word, and prayer. The freedom I desired came a little at a time. Occasionally I still find something from the past hanging on, but I know the way to freedom now, and I refuse to be anything other than free.

If you can relate to my story and are hungry for greater healing and freedom in your life, you may learn some helpful lessons from my books *Healing the Soul of a Woman* and *Beauty for Ashes*.

## The Anatomy of a Control Freak

In his book *The Control Freak*, Les Parrott III lists ten characteristics of a controlling person. One who is controlling is:

- obnoxious
- tenacious
- invasive
- obsessive
- perfectionistic
- critical
- irritable (easily angered)

- demanding
- rigid
- closed-minded

After dealing with several controlling people in my life, I can say amen to all of these characteristics. Notice that the list ends with the observation that controlling people are rigid and closed-minded. Because this is true, they do not allow discussion about anything. Their approach to almost everything is "my way or no way." When others disagree with them, they try to make them feel stupid and inept. I am a communicator, and I like to talk things out. Nothing frustrates me more than trying to talk to people who think they know everything and refuse to open their mind to any opinion besides their own. These are small-minded, prideful, fearful people, yet somehow they think they are strong and powerful.

I have noticed several additional traits of controlling people, which I want to explain and expand upon.

## 1. Controlling people order others around.

People who try to control others do not make polite requests of others. They simply bark orders. Whether they actually have any authority or not, they act as though they are the boss in every situation. They rarely, if ever, say please or thank you. They are demanding, and if anyone mounts even the slightest resistance, they resort to intimidation. They may even threaten ending a relationship, bodily harm, loss of privileges, and other actions they believe would be painful or difficult for the person who will not blindly do as they ask. They often employ the tactics of manipulation and intimidation to help them reach their goal of control.

## 2. Controlling people are volatile when angry.

You never know what will send an angry controller into a rage. When I was young, I could do something one day and my father seemed fine with it, but I could do the same thing the next day and he would become angry about it. I never remember getting to be a child. I don't recall feeling safe, cherished, or protected by either parent, and my father was never proud of me when I did well in school. I was not allowed to have friends except the girl who lived next door, and any mention of a boy sent my father into a rage. When I stop and think about what I went through, I am amazed at God's healing power. When I consider the way I was raised, the fact that I was able to decently parent four children who all serve God and love me with all of their heart can only be attributed to God's grace.

To be fair to my father, I should mention that his father was also controlling and mean. I'm sure that my father endured many negative experiences while growing up and that they contributed a great deal to his behavior as an adult. But being raised in dysfunction can never be an excuse to continue the behavior we witnessed and experienced as young people. My father had a responsibility to break the cycle of abuse and control in which he was raised, but I don't even know if he understood why he was the way he was, nor do I think he cared. In order for people to change, they must want to change.

## 3. Controlling people manipulate by trying to make you feel guilty or as though you owe them something.

I took care of my parents and my aunt in their old age. Dave and I paid for them to live in one of the nicest assisted-living facilities in our city. Eventually they had to go into nursing home care at the same facility due to health issues that could not be managed without skilled care. Often, when I visited my mother, she had a list of items she said she needed, most of which were frivolous, not things she truly needed. On one occasion, I recall her telling me that I was "supposed" to take care of her because she was my mother. This was a rather foolish statement, considering the fact that she never took care of me when my father was abusing me. She was trying to manipulate me by making me feel that I owed her something and trying to make me feel guilty by insinuating I wasn't doing enough for her.

I urge you to be wise enough to recognize these kinds of tactics and resist them wholeheartedly. I took good care of my mother, but had I allowed her to control me, she would have taken up most of my time, and letting her do that would not have been right for me.

> The longer we allow someone to control us, the more difficult it is to break free from their grasp.

I have learned an important lesson about control, and I urge you to remember it: The longer we allow someone to control us, the more difficult it is to break free from their grasp. Staying in a relationship with someone who is controlling allows the fear of that person to become rooted in the very fiber of our being, and it colors or affects everything. My father was extremely controlling, and my fear of him caused me to try to please him when he was unhappy or in a bad mood—or even *appeared* to be upset. I would do almost anything to avoid another violent and explosive blowup in the family. My mother usually tried to avoid him, especially if he was unhappy, which was most of the time, but my default mode was to try to please him.

We cannot live an authentic life and celebrate our uniqueness unless we live in freedom. To embrace who God has made us to be, we must live under the *influence* and *guidance* of the Holy Spirit, not under the *control* of any human being. God wants us to follow *His* will, not the will of other people.

You may have read this chapter and thought about people who have controlled you. You may be able to relate to my story about my controlling father, or you may have a controlling boss, or you may struggle with control in social relationships or in your extended family. Control happens in all kinds of situations. No matter how it has affected your life thus far, there is hope for you. You do not have to live that way, and in the next chapter, I want to help you break free from it.

# CHAPTER 13

# Breaking Free from the Power of Control

*The boundary lines have fallen for me in pleasant places.*

Psalm 16:6

As I wrote in the previous chapter, the longer you allow someone to control you, the more difficult breaking free from them will be. But it is certainly not impossible. If you make up your mind to confront a controller, be assured that they will get angry and begin to blame you for everything. I was about forty-nine years of age before I confronted my father about what he had done to me as a child. His first reaction was rage, but I held my ground. He then tried saying that I wanted him to do the things he did and that I liked them. I told him that the only reason I did everything he wanted was that I was afraid of him. My mother, as usual, hid in another room while I was talking with him. Although I received no apology at that time, I did get the big, dirty family secret out into the open. Things that are hidden in the dark must be exposed to the light in order for freedom and healing to come.

> *Things that are hidden in the dark must be exposed to the light in order for freedom and healing to come.*

A few years later, when I was preparing to go on television and knew that God wanted me to talk openly about my childhood, I felt I should at least inform my father of my intentions. When I told him, he was very quiet, but after a while he said, "Do what you feel you need to do, and don't worry about me." That indicated to me that he felt some remorse, but still no apology came.

My father did eventually apologize to me when he was about eighty years old, and he received Jesus and was baptized. I am thrilled about that, but he missed out on the life he could have enjoyed for years. As an elderly man in poor health, he had nothing but regrets, and he had no one who truly loved him.

When you confront a controller, you may have to face the fact that it could mean the loss of the relationship. One way that controllers operate is to get rid of those who are confronting them; it's part of the way they avoid responsibility for their wrong behavior. When you are willing to work through the problem but the other person won't even consider resolving it, there isn't much you can do in the natural realm. But you can pray, and all things are possible with God (Luke 18:27).

God has called us to peace, and if the person mistreating you refuses to consider changing or getting the help they need, they may decide to break off relationship with you. If they do, it does not necessarily mean that the relationship is over. Sometimes a little time apart gives people time to think and hopefully face the truth. Relationships are important, and I encourage you not to walk away from them without doing everything you can to make them healthy and enjoyable.

Anyone who controls you does not respect you. If you begin to set and keep boundaries in the relationship, the controller may become angry, but hopefully they will respect you. Or you might be in a situation where a friend doesn't respect your boundaries, and if that's the case, then I doubt that person was a true friend in

> *In all your relationships, you have a right and a responsibility to set boundaries.*

the first place. In all your relationships, you have a right and a responsibility to set boundaries in your life and not let people take advantage of you.

Even if both parties in the relationship are willing to work on the problem, it will still be difficult and may take some time. The decision in which you must stand firm is that you will not let them control you any longer. You will have to become accustomed to standing your ground when you feel strongly about something, and the controller will need to learn to not use anger to try to get their way. That means you may have to let them get angry and get over it while you remain firm in your decision. It won't be comfortable for you, not allowing their anger to manipulate you. This will feel new and different to you, because you have allowed it to happen in the past. But the longer you stand firm, the easier it will be.

## The Controller Gets Confronted

People who have controlled me include my father, one employer, and one friend. But oddly enough, I not only allowed people to control me, but I also controlled others. I was a controller in my home and with people who were not as aggressive as I was. My wonderful husband is a peace lover, and he let me behave badly without confronting me for many years. In certain ways, I secretly wanted him to confront me, but in other ways, if he dared to try, I reacted to him as my father did to me. I became angry and blamed him for my unhappiness.

The human race in general is very messed up, and I am amazed that God is so long-suffering with us. He understands us and not only sees what we do but knows why we do it, and in my case the reason was twofold. I wanted to be in control because I wasn't convinced that anyone would ever have my best interests in mind, so I took care of myself. I was also very selfish, but then most of us are, until we allow God to work in us. I didn't know I was selfish, nor did I realize I was being controlling. I thought I was keeping things going the way they should go, not realizing that my way wasn't always the right way.

Dave did eventually confront me, and I believe the Holy Spirit led him concerning the timing and the way in which he did it. When the time was right, he confronted me about my behavior, and he has never backed down since then. Had he done it sooner, I might have simply left him. I still had many unresolved issues from my past and might have been unable to stay committed to the relationship in the face of honest confrontation. When I had received a good measure of healing from God, I knew my behavior was wrong, but I doubt I would have ever changed it without some confrontation. By confronting me, Dave possibly helped me even more than he helped himself.

I remember feeling the rage and rebellion inside of me when Dave told me that he simply wasn't going to put up with my behavior any longer. He said that either I could change or, in time, he might not be able to stand being around me. Had it not been for the fact that I loved the Lord so much, I am sure I would have done something desperate, but the truth was that I did want to change—I just didn't know how to do it.

All I knew to do was to be open to the Holy Spirit. He put just the right books in my hands at the right time and taught me some much-needed truths from them. In addition, God's grace was active in my life, helping me to change. And I am thankful to say that I finally did change. I have a strong personality, and I can't say I don't like to be right, because I do, but I refuse to argue about it anymore or to cause strife in my life in order to be right.

| *Being right is highly overrated.* |

Being right is highly overrated anyway. The smug feeling it gives us lasts only a very short time.

I am appalled now when I look back at situations that caused me to boil in anger for days—days that are now lost forever. As we gain experience in life, we usually learn that what we thought was important wasn't important

| *Letting God change us is much better than trying to change someone else.* |

at all, and that issues we ignored were the ones worth paying attention to. Letting God change us is much better than trying to change someone else. Search your heart and ask God to reveal to you how much time you waste being upset about petty situations and to show you how much better it would be to simply let them go.

Trying to control everything and everyone around us is hard work, and I have no desire to do it any longer. I desire right relationship with God, peace, and joy. And I am willing to give up anything else in order to have those blessings.

## Balance

I feel that I need to say that not all control is wrong. God is a God of order, and He establishes lines of authority that are to be respected. We are not being controlled every time someone asks us to do something we don't want to do or says something with which we don't agree.

Women supposedly have been liberated, but the desire not to be controlled has led many to become rebellious controllers themselves. Believe it or not, I am a submissive wife. Just this week Dave wanted to do something I did not agree with. I stated my opinion, and I felt—and still feel—that I was right. But he was firm in what he wanted to do. I asked him to pray about it for one day and told him that I would accept whatever conclusion he reached. In the meantime, I asked God to guide him. When he came back to me, he still felt the same way, so I said, "Then let's do it," and I wasn't angry or resentful at all. We must always remember that simply *thinking* we are right doesn't mean that we are.

Let me be quick to share that in my relationship with Dave, there are times when I feel very strongly about a situation and the two of us disagree about it. When that happens, we agree to wait until we can find a middle ground where we can both be content and feel we have made the right decision.

> *We must always remember that simply thinking we are right doesn't mean that we are.*

Let me summarize this chapter and the previous one with this simple advice: Don't allow yourself to be controlled, don't be a controller, and always, always seek balance. Without balance, you will gain freedom in one area but may create a problem in another.

Let me also encourage you again to be submissive to the authority over you unless those people demand that you do something that you believe would offend God. Finally, ask the Holy Spirit to guide you regarding when to confront a situation and when to wait. As you move toward confrontation, pray about it and ask the Holy Spirit to lead you as you do it. I also suggest that you never confront anyone without having first asked God to prepare the person's heart so they will sincerely listen to what you have to say, and pray that you will speak wisely and calmly.

This book is about being authentic and unique, and we certainly cannot be authentic (sincere) if we react out of fear rather than out of our heart's desire. The more we break the power of other people's control in our lives, the more we are free to be who God has made us to be and to pursue the hopes and dreams He has put in our hearts.

# CHAPTER 14

# You Can't Please Everyone, Part 1

*Don't worry about who doesn't like you, who has more, or who's doing what.*

Erma Bombeck

Although I have mentioned the dangers of being people-pleasers already in this book, the topic deserves an entire chapter because it is a problem with which many people struggle. Some people are people-pleasers and don't realize it, while others believe pleasing the people around them is a godly way to behave. I say, by all means be a blessing to people and don't live a self-centered life, but don't let your efforts to please others control you, cause you to disobey God, or steal the life God has specially designed for you.

Jesus "made Himself of no reputation" (Philippians 2:7 NKJV). This means that He did what His Father in heaven wanted Him to do, not what people wanted Him to do. He simply was not concerned about His reputation (what people thought about Him). His own brothers were ashamed of Him and tried to motivate Him to do something amazing to prove He was the Messiah, but He told them His time had not yet come (John 7:4–6). They thought He was out of His mind (Mark 3:21), but because His goal was to please God, not Himself or other people, He was free from the tyranny of worrying about what people thought of Him.

He was completely secure in the love of His Father, and that kind of security makes a person bold and courageous.

The apostle Paul said that had he tried to be popular with people, he would not have become a "servant of Christ" (Galatians 1:10). We can see from this verse that people-pleasing can derail our destiny. I think it is safe to say that if we want to fully follow God, we have to be willing to displease some people sometimes.

*People-pleasing can derail our destiny.*

I think most of the great men and women we read about in the Bible had to face this challenge of displeasing people in order to please God. Doing so is a key to spiritual growth, and I encourage you to ask yourself if you are willing to do that if it becomes necessary.

Paul also said that he and his ministry companions had been "approved by God to be entrusted with the gospel. We are not trying to please people but God, who tests our hearts" (1 Thessalonians 2:4). Anyone who speaks the gospel message has probably had to face this test of choosing to please God rather than fellow human beings. As a Bible teacher, I know that I cannot preach to please people, but I must say what God wants me to say, even if it isn't what people want to hear.

The Bible teaches us that a time will come when people will not tolerate sound doctrine. "Instead, to suit their own desires, they will gather around them a great number of teachers to say what their itching ears want to hear" (2 Timothy 4:3). I believe that time is upon us. I am committed to teaching what I believe people need to hear, not merely what they want to hear.

Jesus preached many truths that people didn't want to hear and never compromised His message in order to get people to like Him. We cannot compromise our message, either.

I wonder how many people are growing and doing well in their relationship with God end up backing down because of criticism? John wrote that many of the leading Jews believed in Jesus, but they would not openly acknowl-edge their faith because they were afraid the Pharisees would put them out of the synagogue (John 12: 42–43). They were afraid of rejec-tion from the people they wanted to accept them. As long as our reputation is too important to us, we will not be able to be authentic or unique. If what other people think of us matters too much, we will pretend to be something we are not in order to avoid the pain of rejection.

> As long as our reputation is too important to us, we will not be able to be authentic or unique.

I love the old saying about being too concerned with other people's opinions: "You wouldn't worry so much about what oth-ers think of you if you realized how seldom they do." Critical people will find something to criticize about you, no matter what you do, so why not go ahead and follow your heart and live a life worth living, a life you will enjoy?

## Your Self-Image

Your self-image is like a picture of yourself that you carry inside of you. What do you think of yourself? Do you like yourself? Do you know who you are in Christ Jesus? Do you appreciate your uniqueness? Do you appreciate your capabilities? Are you overly concerned with what people think of you? Do you believe you are a person worth knowing? All of the answers to these questions and others like them can help you truly know what your self-image is.

If you are constantly waiting for someone else to tell you that you are acceptable and that you have worth and value, you may have many unhappy days throughout your life, because people won't always do what you would like them to do.

As long as you need others to keep you propped up concerning how you feel about yourself, you will never be free from people-pleasing. If your self-image is not good, then God wants to help you change it. He wants to be your friend, but He also wants you to be a friend to yourself. You begin that friendship by deciding to value and accept yourself.

> *Trying to be first in everything in life takes a lot of energy and quickly becomes exhausting.*

Many people struggle to be first in everything because they think that makes them valuable or well thought of. They cannot even enjoy playing a game because they have to win to feel acceptable. Their focus is on beating everyone else, not on having fun. Trying to be first in everything in life takes a lot of energy and quickly becomes exhausting. No wonder Jesus tells us that "the last will be first, and the first will be last" (Matthew 20:16). If we are overly competitive and resentful or jealous when others win or experience blessings, we will ultimately fail. But, if we are glad when others succeed and feel no need to try to get ahead of them, we will be blessed. I believe that being happy for others who succeed is an important key to our own success. God promotes people with kind and generous hearts, not those with jealous and envious hearts.

There is nothing wrong with wanting to do your best, but an attitude that drives you to be better than others in order to be satisfied does not please God. He loves you as a person, but He does not love that kind of attitude. When your self-image is what God wants it to be, you will have no need to be first always or to be better than others. You already know that you are first with God because we are all the apple of His eye. God doesn't have a few favorites. We are all His favorite!

Why struggle to gain acceptance and approval from others since God is offering it to you freely? God accepts you. God approves of you. God loves you with a perfect love. Don't struggle trying to get something you already have.

## Five Sure Signs of a People-Pleaser

### 1. *A people-pleaser lives to gain approval through pleasing others.*

Are you living to please yourself, other people, or God? Hopefully, your answer is God, because living to please anyone else never ends happily. Paul wrote to the Colossians that everything we do should be done for the Lord, not for other people, knowing that in living that way, we will receive an inheritance from the Lord (Colossians 3: 23–24).

Jesus taught that we should not do anything from impure motives of trying to please or impress other people. This is what I would call a deeper-life teaching, because unveiling our motives requires us to be still and quiet and ask ourselves some hard questions. We have to go to a deep place inside of ourselves to think about our motives and, if they are not godly, to either change our motives or stop doing what we have been doing.

*People-pleasing can stunt a person's spiritual growth.*

People-pleasing can stunt a person's spiritual growth. For example, God may want to take you into a deeper, more committed area with Him, somewhere your friends don't want to go. What will your choice be? Are you willing to lose friends if necessary in order to go deeper with God? Are you ready to lose your reputation with people if that's what it takes in order to live a life that is pleasing to God? Often, when people are fully committed to God they will be called "Jesus freaks," "Bible-thumpers," "holy rollers," or "fanatics." But let's remember that Jesus was jeered at, spat upon, told He was crazy, called a fanatic and a false prophet, accused of working with the devil, rejected, hated, and crucified. He said that if people hated Him, they would also hate us (John 15:18), so we should not be surprised when our choices to grow in relationship with Him are not popular with others or even cause them to mock or ridicule us.

If you are willing to lose some friends in order to follow God's will and leading in your life, He will provide friends who love you, true friends who won't turn against you when you need them most. He will be your best Friend, and that is more important than anything else. On your journey to be authentic and unique, seek friends who are also authentic and unique.

Jesus sent seventy people, in pairs of two, to minister for Him in various towns. He told them that if those to whom they tried to minister did not receive them, they should shake the dust off of their feet and move on to another town (Luke 10:1–17). Though Jesus gave this advice thousands of years ago,

> Don't let rejection stop you; just shake it off and keep going.

it is an excellent guideline for you and me today. Don't let rejection stop you; just shake it off and keep going.

## 2. A people-pleaser does not have realistic expectations.

Everyone has expectations, but you are only one person, and you cannot do what everyone expects you to do. We juggle many different relationships in life, and each person wants something different from us. Your elderly parents may want you to visit more, or you may be their caregiver. Your children want your time and attention. Your spouse wants you to do a variety of things. Friends need favors, they want phone calls, or they want you to attend their barbecue. Your place of employment wants you to give them your best forty hours a week and sometimes even more. Your child's school wants you to volunteer. The neighborhood association wants you to be on the board so you can help make decisions. The list is seemingly endless.

For someone who has not learned to say no when needed, the expectations of others become a problem. However, saying no is very hard for some of us, and for others it is impossible, because they need approval much more than they should. We should all say yes to some opportunities and no to other opportunities, but not automatically accept or reject every request.

We may also have expectations of other people, and they do not always meet those expectations. If we need them to say yes to our every request in order to feel good about ourselves, we will be unhappy much of the time. For example, I might go to a wedding reception expecting the mother of the bride to spend time talking with me. When the party is over, she hasn't even said hello. If I don't have a good self-image and am addicted to approval, I may suffer emotionally for days about something she failed to do and didn't even know I expected.

Just because I expect someone to do something doesn't mean the person is obligated to do it. When someone expects something from me, I am not obligated to do that, either. We would all be so much happier if we would put our expectations in God instead of people, trusting Him to give us what He knows we need. He may not give us exactly what we want, but if not, He will give us something far better.

Moses expected the Israelites to understand that God had sent him to deliver them from slavery, but they did not understand (Acts 7:25). I'm sure Joseph expected his brothers to be happy for him when his father gave him the special coat he made for him, but they were not happy. They were bitter, resentful, and jealous (Genesis 37:3–4).

There have been times when my expectations were not met and it left me disappointed or even angry, but that was my own fault. The person I was angry with may not have even known what I expected. If we are secure, then we can make our expectations known in order to discover whether the other person wants to or is able to meet them. An example would be to say to the mother of the bride, "Will you be able to spend some time at the reception talking with me?" Then she will know your expectation. That way she can let you know ahead of time that she might be too busy but that your being there would still mean a lot to her.

We need to be able to do good deeds for people without having any expectation other than to make them happy. If we need to be noticed, appreciated, and applauded every time we do an act of kindness, then we are insecure people-pleasers rather than God-pleasers.

## 3. A people-pleaser sets aside their own legitimate needs.

We all have needs, and although we should not live self-centered lives, neither should we deny all of our needs in an effort to please everyone else. If we do, we will eventually resent it, and the situation may become explosive.

People-pleasers may recognize their needs and even vocalize them but still keep denying them in order to please someone else. They become martyrs—people who live to please others and then resent it and complain about how much people use them and how little anyone does for them.

I encourage you to live a balanced life in this area. Do things for others when you feel peace about doing them. At the same time, also realize that you have needs and if you don't meet them, eventually you won't have anything left to give. That will open a door for the devil to bring misery into your life (1 Peter 5:8).

My daughter Laura is a great example of maintaining balance in this area. She helps me in many ways and feels called to do so. She is a very flexible woman, and most of the time I can call and ask, "What are you doing?" and she will reply, "What do you want me to do?" She does almost anything I ask her to do, but there are times when she says, "No, I'm sorry, but I can't do that because we have family plans," or "I'm already overloaded," or something else. She and I have an agreement to be honest with each other at all times. I want her to always be free to say no if that is what she needs to say.

If you find yourself doing things for others and complaining about it, even in the privacy of your own mind, then you may be a people-pleaser. If you decide to do something for another person, do it with a good attitude so your actions will please God.

## 4. A people-pleaser feels awful when their decisions do not please other people.

God's Word teaches us that we must obey God rather than other human beings (Acts 5:29), and this is an important scripture for us to heed. God wants us to follow His guidance, but people usually want us to do what will benefit them. That doesn't make them bad people; it just means they are human.

When someone asks us to do something, that person never wants to hear us say no. If we say we cannot do it, their initial response may not be positive, but that is between them and God. Their bad reaction is not our responsibility. However, people-pleasers wrongly assume responsibility for other people's emotional reactions, such as anger, unhappiness, or disappointment, and they often adjust their own behavior to whatever will keep the other person happy. In doing this, they are allowing those people to control them with their emotions.

> We must beware of having a false sense of responsibility.

A spiritually mature person learns to deal with disappointment with a good attitude while trusting God. We must beware of having a false sense of responsibility. If we cannot give people what they want because we feel we are following God's will for us, it is not our fault if they are unhappy.

## 5. A people-pleaser is dishonest.

Referring to people-pleasers as dishonest may sound harsh, but they do have a pattern of not being honest about their desires, feelings, and thoughts. They tell people what they want to hear instead of telling them the truth. They have a bad habit of saying yes when they really know they should say no. I know this because I certainly did it in the earlier years of my life.

People-pleasing behavior is quite dishonorable. Paul wrote to the Ephesians that they should let their lives "lovingly express truth [in all things, speaking truly, dealing truly, living truly]" (Ephesians 4:15 AMPC). The fact that someone may not want to hear the truth and could even be offended by it does not relieve us of the responsibility to speak it.

If you have been a people-pleaser and are now ready to change, you can expect resistance from your friends and family in the beginning. They are accustomed to getting you to do their bidding. Be kind and give them time. Don't go to the opposite extreme, where you never want to do anything for them or sacrifice your own pleasure for them, but remain steady. As time goes by, you will enter into more balanced and healthy relationships. If people don't want to be friends with you because they can no longer control you, then they were never true friends anyway, and you haven't lost anything that was worth keeping.

# CHAPTER 15

# You Can't Please Everyone, Part 2

*The price of greatness is responsibility.*

Winston Churchill

In order to please everyone, you must meet certain requirements. If you were fully aware of what it really takes to please the people around you, you might choose not to do it. Let's look at some of those requirements, and then you can decide if having everyone be pleased with you is worth what it costs you.

## Four Requirements of People-Pleasing

### 1. *People-pleasing requires us to disrespect ourselves.*

We respect others because they are honest, genuine, authentic, and real. They are trustworthy. We need to meet the same requirements if we are to respect ourselves.

If I say yes to someone's request when my heart is screaming no, then I am not being true to myself. Therefore, I forfeit some of my self-respect. There is no better feeling than to lay your head down at night and know that you are following your heart in life. You are doing as you believe God would have you do. And there is no worse feeling than to lay your head down at night and be

tormented with feelings of guilt because you know you committed to something you dread doing and, in fact, don't believe you
should be doing. I'm sure you have heard the saying "A man must
be able to look at himself in the mirror and like what he sees." If
we feel ashamed when we look in the mirror because we know
we have been too cowardly to say no when we needed to, then we
have sacrificed our self-respect.

Feelings of guilt that never go away can be the cause of mental
illness. I once visited a mental institution attempting to do some
ministry with the patients, and what I saw was very sad. In an
area where some of the most difficult patients were kept, I saw
people walking around in zombie-like states. Some were clutch-
ing crucifixes they wore around their neck and repeating over
and over, "It's my fault. Everything is my fault."

They had carried heavy burdens of guilt for so long that it drove
them mad. I mentioned in an earlier chapter that my mother knew
that my father was abusing me sexually, and she did nothing about
it. I could tell from what she said sometimes that she felt terribly
guilty. Eventually, she had a mental breakdown and received two
years of shock treatments, because that was the preferred protocol
at the time. The woman I knew as my mother disappeared during
those years, and she was never the same after that treatment.

She had no self-respect because of what she allowed my father
to do to me. She was afraid of him and tried to please him, no matter what the cost. But she sacrificed her life and mental health, in
addition to doing a great deal of damage to her relationship with
my brother and me. My father's abuse and my mother's abandon-
ing me when I needed her most left me wounded and broken.
I thank God for the healing and restoration that I have experienced in my life. Let me encourage you: No matter what you have

done or what people have done to you, God is ready to restore you and heal all the wounded and broken places in your life.

## 2. People-pleasing requires us to be responsible for things that are not our responsibility.

My husband is not responsible for my joy, but for many years I blamed him if I wasn't happy. I expected everyone in my family to live their lives to please me, and I wasn't even aware I was doing it. I grew up with the expectation that they should please me because that's what my father expected of me, and I continued that behavior because it was all I knew.

> My joy is my own responsibility.

Thank God, He taught me differently. I grew spiritually and learned that my joy is my responsibility; to put that responsibility on anyone else is unfair to the other person. Of course, we should live to help others and desire to make them happy, but not at the expense of taking on a responsibility that is not ours to take.

Parents who think it is their responsibility to make sure their sons and daughters are happy all the time often end up with entitled, manipulative children. It is good for everyone to not get their way all the time. It helps us learn to deal with disappointment without losing our joy. Some of the best lessons we can teach our children are to be responsible, to work hard in life, and to appreciate everything they are given. It is also good for them to experience the consequences of wrong choices. If we always deliver them from discomfort, then we fail to teach them to deal with real life, which includes trials, difficulties, and disappointments.

> It is good for everyone to not get their way all the time.

Tony was very controlling. His wife, Lauren, needed his permission to spend any money, to spend time with friends, and even to go to church. He rarely gave her permission. Because she was a people-pleaser, she always said that whatever he wanted was fine. Eventually, she began to resent him but pretended to love him. As time went by, she resented him more and more, until she began to despise him. One day while he was at work, she packed her clothes and left him. She later divorced him. However, had Lauren confronted Tony's controlling behavior early in their relationship, they might have enjoyed a good marriage. He was wrong to control her, but she was equally as wrong to allow him to do so, because it was her responsibility to protect her basic God-given right to make decisions for her life.

### 3. People-pleasing requires us to have unhealthy relationships.

If we imagine that it is our responsibility to keep people happy all the time by saying yes to whatever they want us to do, then we have a false sense of responsibility. Our number one responsibility is to be obedient to God above all else. If we are obedient to Him, then everything else in our life will be right. He guides us in all areas of daily living, including how to navigate all of our relationships. For example, a few years back I realized I had a lot of relationships in which I did all the giving and the other person did all the taking. When God opened my eyes, I realized that those relationships were not healthy for me or the other people, and I started making changes. I want relationships that are fulfilling to me as well as to the other person, and we have no real relationship unless we do things for each other.

Jesus was washing His disciples' feet, and when He came to

Peter, he told Jesus, "You shall never wash my feet." Jesus replied, "Unless I wash you, you have no part with me" (John 13:8). I think this one scripture proves the point that for relationships to be true, healthy relationships, they must involve give and take. Now is a good time to take a look at all of your relationships and ask God to show you if any of them are unhealthy. If so, there is no better time than now to begin setting them right.

If we say yes to people too often, we begin to resent them for taking advantage of us. We need to realize that we can say no if we are willing to have people be displeased with us. If we are people-pleasers—if we care too much about what people think of us or we are overly concerned about our reputation—then we are destined for unhealthy relationships that are never fulfilling to us.

> To be authentic, we must be bold enough to speak the truth in love.

## 4. People-pleasing requires us to be phony instead of authentic.

We tell people we like things that we don't really like, and we agree to do things that we don't want to do. To be authentic, we must be bold enough to speak the truth in love (Ephesians 4:15). We regularly find ourselves in situations when we must decide whether or not we will be authentic or compromise our heart in order to tell people what we know will make them feel good. I am dealing with two situations right now that require me to find a way to be honest with a person and yet not hurt their feelings. It isn't easy, but I am committed to being authentic, so I will have to find a way to do it with God's help. I will do everything I can do to avoid hurting them, but ultimately, if they get their feelings hurt because I am obeying God, it is their problem, not mine.

I want to repeat this because it is very important: We should want to please people in a healthy, balanced way. We should not be selfish, expecting to always get our own way. We should do some things we don't want to do as long as we know that doing them is the right thing to do, but we should not let the fear of other people's reactions control us or let pleasing people become the most important focus of our lives.

## The Price of Greatness

Winston Churchill said the price of greatness is responsibility, but when we please people instead of God, we turn our backs on our responsibility to Him. We have a responsibility to be truthful with people.

> We have a responsibility to be truthful with people.

An extremely difficult aspect of leadership is knowing that no matter what decision you make, some people probably won't like it. Trying to please everyone can complicate or hinder your decision-making, so let me urge you to be true to your own heart and to what God is calling you to do. Let those who don't like it deal with it between themselves and God. There is a price to pay for greatness, and that price is doing what you are responsible for doing, even if doesn't make you popular with the people around you.

Jesus says that if we are persecuted for righteousness' sake, we are blessed (Matthew 5:10). We don't feel very blessed during the persecution, but the joy we gain from knowing we are doing the right thing and being in the center of God's will is worth being judged, criticized, misunderstood, or rejected.

I shudder when I think of what I would have missed had I tried to please people instead of doing what I knew in my heart was right for me when God called me into ministry. Let me ask you: Have you missed great opportunities due to people-pleasing? I strongly encourage you to never trade your opportunity to do something great for applause from people. People who want you to follow them instead of following your own heart don't really care about you anyway. We should encourage others to follow their heart and be led by the Spirit of God instead of insisting that they do what we want them to do in order to keep our friendship, and we should surround ourselves with people who do the same for us.

> Have you missed great opportunities due to people-pleasing?

## It's Never Too Late to Change

I have some really good news to share with you: If you have been a people-pleaser or a less-than-authentic person, it is never too late to change. You can decide today that no matter what it costs, you will do your best to follow your heart instead of people. If you have allowed someone else to make your decisions for you, and it has been that way for a long time, making a change won't be easy, but you can do it.

When you need to make an adjustment in a relationship I recommend a three-step process:

### 1. Have a conversation.

Sit down with the person and let them know that you realize you have made a mistake by doing what they wanted you to do instead of following your heart. Communicate clearly that you need to change the dynamics of the relationship. Don't accuse them or tell them what they have done wrong, because that will put the other person on the defensive and perhaps even make them angry.

## 2. Communicate clearly and responsibly.

Take responsibility for your part in the unhealthy relationship, and let the person know specifically what you need from them in the future.

## 3. Assess the response.

If the person is unwilling to change, then learn how to say no and stick to it. This may be hard for you to do at first, but think about what you will be giving up if you continue in your old pattern. You may lose a friend, but if someone has to control you to be your friend, then that person is not a true friend at all, and you won't have lost much.

Pray for and seek healthy relationships—or we might even say "safe" relationships, ones in which you will be respected and given the privilege of being honest about your desires. Make a commitment to be your most authentic and unique self, and search for friends who will allow you that freedom.

> Make a commitment to be your most authentic and unique self.

God wants you to enjoy a happy life. That simply isn't possible unless you follow His guidance and can truly be yourself.

CHAPTER 16

# Overcoming the Fear of Rejection

*Whoever listens to you listens to me; whoever rejects you
rejects me; but whoever rejects me rejects him who sent me.*

Luke 10:16

One reason people hesitate to be authentic and embrace their uniqueness and share it with others is that they fear they will be rejected if they do. According to an article on *Business Insider*, "Researchers found that the same areas of our brain light up in an MRI machine when we experience rejection as when we experience physical pain. That's why rejection can feel like a punch in the gut, or a knife to the heart; you're literally using the same part of the brain as when you hurt yourself physically."

I believe that our enemy, the devil, uses rejection possibly more than anything else to try to stop us from making progress in various ous areas of our lives, to keep us from doing what God wants us to do, and to prevent us from living as our authentic selves. Rejection is extremely painful, and those who have experienced it work hard to avoid it in the future. The fear of rejection is often the root cause of people-pleasing.

> The fear of rejection is often the root cause of people-pleasing.

When Jesus sent His disciples out two by two to preach the gospel, heal the sick, and cast out demons, He warned them that they would be rejected and instructed them to shake off the rejection and move on to the next town (Luke 9:1–5; 10:1–11). Jesus was rejected and even hated without a cause (John 15:25), and He told us that we would experience the same kind of treatment. He said that the student is not above his master and that if people persecuted or rejected Him, they will also persecute or reject us (John 15:20). I don't think it is possible to get through life without experiencing rejection somewhere along the way.

You may have been rejected for a promotion at work, a job for which you applied, a role in the school play, or a place in the band or on the cheerleading squad. Friends or family may reject you if you decide to do something they don't agree with. In a marriage, one partner may reject the other in order to be with someone else.

Some people are more sensitive to rejection than others are, but I don't know of anyone who likes and enjoys it. Some of the worst pain in my life has come from rejection, and I have definitely had some experiences of rejection that have taught me how the devil uses it to derail us as we try to move forward in life.

One thing you can be sure of is that God will never reject you (John 6:37). Knowing this truth brings us great comfort. God's love is everlasting, and no matter how many times we fail, He never rejects us when we come to Him.

> One thing you can be sure of is that God will never reject you.

I started out in life being rejected as a daughter—by my father—and being received only as an object of his sexual desires. My mother rejected me when she abandoned me to his abuse rather than protecting me and keeping me safe. I married the first boy who showed any interest in me because I was afraid no one else would ever want me. I was eighteen years old at the time, and on several occasions, my husband abandoned me for other women, so I experienced serious rejection from him. Eventually we divorced, and thankfully I met and married Dave, who has loved me at all times. However, when we married, I was so wounded from the abuse and rejection in my past that it took me years to learn to accept and trust Dave's love for me.

I had a root (a deeply entrenched belief) of rejection in my soul, which caused me to expect rejection and even imagine I was being rejected when I wasn't. The night Dave asked me to marry him, he said, "I want to talk to you about something," and I was sure he wanted to break up with me. I always expected the worst, so imagine my surprise when he asked me to marry him instead!

After Dave and I married, we experienced many frustrations because anytime he so much as disagreed with me, I felt rejected. I had to learn that he could reject my opinion and not be rejecting me at all. He didn't understand why I behaved as I did, and I didn't, either. He felt he couldn't have his own opinion without my becoming angry. When he didn't agree with me, I did get angry, and that anger stemmed from old, misplaced feelings of rejection. I finally learned that my opinion is totally separate from who I am as a person and that people may not like what I like, but they can still like me.

Dave and I had been married about nine years when God called me to teach His Word, and I had no idea how much rejection awaited me over the next few years. I mentioned earlier that friends and family rejected Dave and me when I started leading a Bible study in our home because I was the one teaching it. They thought Dave should teach, and that a woman had no right to do so. Their rejection was not cryptic or covert. Our friends from church said plainly, "If this is what you plan to do, then we can't have anything to do with you." Ouch! This brought me into an intense experience with the fear of man, which is a biblical term for being afraid of what other people think, say, or do. I had a decision to make: Would I please the people or please God? Obviously, I couldn't do both, so I chose God, and I am very glad I did. I did lose those friends, but eventually God replaced them with others who encouraged me to follow Him.

## The Fear of Man

When we live in the fear of man and do as other people want us to do instead of what God wants us to do, it becomes a trap for us. Proverbs 29:25 says, "Fear of man will prove to be a snare, but whoever trusts in the Lord is kept safe." Our enemy, Satan, uses the fear of what other people will think, say, or do to draw us into his trap, which is filled with various kinds of agony and misery for us.

Saul, the great and powerful king of Israel, became ensnared in the fear of man and lost his kingdom because of it. His is a sad story, but it is also a good example of what happens when we listen to people and do what they want us to do instead of listening to God.

The prophet Samuel instructed Saul to make a sacrifice to God (a burnt offering and a peace offering) when threatened by the mighty Philistine army. He specifically told Saul to wait seven days before making it. But because the people became impatient and began to abandon Saul, he made the sacrifice prematurely (1 Samuel 13:8–12).

In 1 Samuel 15:3, God gave Saul another instruction for battle through Samuel, saying: "Now go, attack the Amalekites and totally destroy all that belongs to them. Do not spare them; put to death men and women, children and infants, cattle and sheep, camels and donkeys." Saul did *most* of what God told him to do, but he and the army "spared Agag and the best of the sheep and cattle, the fat calves and lambs—everything that was good. These they were unwilling to destroy completely, but everything that was despised and weak they totally destroyed" (1 Samuel 15:9).

When the Lord confronted Saul about his rebellion and told him that He regretted making him king (1 Samuel 15:10–11), Saul made one excuse after another for his behavior, to the point of saying he had only kept the best of everything in order to sacrifice it to the Lord. Why did Saul behave this way? When Samuel asked him about it, he admitted that his fear of people had caused him to disobey God and said: "I have sinned. I violated the Lord's command and your instructions. I was afraid of the men and so I gave in to them" (1 Samuel 15:24).

We can easily see that Saul feared man and cared more about what people thought and did than about God. If we think about this rationally, we wonder, why do we care so much about what people think of us? After all, their thoughts cannot really hurt us. If we lose relationships with people because we refuse to cower under their demands, they are not worth our investment of time anyway.

> Why do we care so much about what people think of us?

## A Curiosity

It is curious to me that people who have deep wounds from rejection often become very successful, even becoming government and world leaders. Often, their desire to prove that they are of value drives them to work so hard that they excel in their fields. They become super achievers and high performers. According to Paul Tournier's book *Creative Suffering*, "As many as three-fourths of the most celebrated high achievers have come from backgrounds of abuse and severe mistreatment."

He goes on to say that these people will practically work themselves to death to prove they have worth and value. I know these symptoms because for years I was also driven to be successful due to the abuse during my childhood. I recall my father telling me that I would never amount to anything, and I was determined to prove him wrong. Thankfully, God helped me purify my motives before I made too many mistakes, but I did manage to make myself very ill on a few occasions simply from the stress of seeking my worth and value through work. I still work hard, but now I do it for the right reasons, and I live a balanced life.

In my book *The Root of Rejection*, I include a story about a man named David Brainerd. His father died when he was eight years old, and his mother passed away when he was fourteen. Even though he inherited a sizable estate, he was denied love and affection, which is vital to a child's sense of happiness and security.

Brainerd became a missionary to a Native American tribe, the Delaware Indians in New Jersey. His life was filled with difficulty, and throughout his life he carried an unusual burden of guilt, as though he felt responsible for his parents' deaths. The Holy Spirit repeatedly tried to teach David that his sufficiency was in Christ. He seemed to understand that truth for a while, only to lose sight of it again and revert to works-oriented religion, which caused him to suffer unbearably as he tried to perfect himself. David Brainerd's health broke down under the stress in his life, and he died at the age of twenty-nine from tuberculosis. Even though he had a powerful ministry, he became an invalid. He completely exhausted himself trying to serve God perfectly.

I wonder, how many David Brainerds are there in the world today? How many people exhaust themselves day after day, trying to achieve success in order to prove they are worth something?

## Rooted in God's Love and Acceptance

There is only one infallible lesson we can learn that will make us immune to the agony of rejection: God loves us unconditionally. We are to be deeply rooted in God's love, according to Ephesians 3:17. Anything that is deeply rooted cannot be uprooted by the storms of life. When our roots are in Christ and in His love and acceptance, we can withstand rejection. We may not like being rejected, but rejection will not defeat us. As Romans 8:31 says, "If God is for us, who can be against us?" (NKJV). And the psalmist writes in Psalm 118:6, "The Lord is with me; I will not be afraid. What can mere mortals do to me?"

It takes time for our old thinking to be renewed and for us to learn to think as beloved children of God, but it can happen if we stick to believing God's Word rather than our own conflicted feelings.

*When our roots are in Christ, we can withstand rejection.*

If the foundation of your life is rejection rather than acceptance, you may perceive you are being rejected when that is not the case at all. You could walk into a room of people, and if someone doesn't pay attention to you right away, you might assume that no one likes you and feel rejected. In a group setting, you can join in the conversation, but if you fear rejection, you won't take the chance of being rejected, so you will sit back and wait for everyone else to make you feel accepted. The truth is that God loves you unconditionally, and based on that, you can build your life on His love and total acceptance of you rather than on rejection.

## A Lesson Learned

One Sunday, I was having a particularly hard time. I was in my home office crying, but not sure what I was crying about. We had just returned from a ministry trip, and I was very tired, so I am sure the fatigue affected the way I was feeling. Dave walked into my office to tell me goodbye because he was leaving to play golf, and part of my problem was that I felt sorry for myself because he was going to have fun, and all I had to do was stay home alone and be bored. (Poor me!) He asked me why I was crying and if I wanted to talk about anything, and I told him, "No, not now."

As we talked about the situation later, he asked me why I didn't simply ask him to stay home and spend time with me. I had no answer because I didn't know why I didn't ask. As I prayed about it, God showed me that I didn't ask because I was afraid Dave would say no, and I would feel rejected. I wonder how often the fear of being rejected prevents us from doing what we would like to do or saying what we would like to say? I'm sure it is more often than we may realize.

A foundation of rejection makes a person insecure, and insecurity is a tormenting condition that can only be cured by God's unconditional love. Insecure people exist in the shadows of life because they would rather hide than live in the open and be honest about their desires and needs. To be authentic, we need to be healed from the fear of rejection and from insecurity, and God is an expert at healing these painful emotional conditions. All you need to do to receive healing is open your heart and invite Him into every area of your life, especially the ones you have kept hidden. Healing does involve some pain, simply because we have to confront issues from which we have previously hidden, but the pain ultimately moves us toward freedom and away from an endless, empty ache.

We have to take chances and step out into the world, realizing that everyone won't accept us, but keeping in mind that we already have the acceptance of the most important person in our lives—Jesus. The devil will use the fear of rejection to keep us isolated if we allow him to do so, but why would we do that when freedom is available?

You are God's beloved, and He has great plans for you, so tighten your seat belt and get ready for the journey toward love and freedom.

# CHAPTER 17

# Authenticity Requires Integrity

*The integrity of the upright guides them, but the unfaithful are destroyed by their duplicity.*

Proverbs 11:3

Oxford Languages defines *integrity* as "the quality of being honest and having strong moral principles; moral uprightness; the state of being whole and undivided." In other words, a person with integrity sees no difference between their behavior and what their inmost being approves of. They only do what their conscience allows them to do. They are always honest, and they keep their word.

> A person with integrity sees no difference between their behavior and what their inmost being approves of.

Integrity is very important to me because it is a foundational principle on which we have built our ministry. God told us to always do what we said we would do, and to be honest with the money that passes through our hands. We have endeavored to do both, and we will continue to do so.

Proverbs teaches us over and over that a business managed according to the principles of integrity (faithfulness) will prosper and be successful (Proverbs 28:20). Think about this: A business owner decides to reduce the quality of his merchandise just a little and still charge the same price for it, thinking that he will make more money. He feels a bit uncomfortable in his spirit about doing it, but he reasons that it is only a little and everyone does it, so why shouldn't he do it, too? He talks himself into doing what he knows is wrong if he were to be totally honest with himself, but he manages to ignore the gnawing feeling in his spirit until it goes away. Let's say that a year or two go by, and sure enough, his profits have been larger and everything seems to be going well. He feels confident that, since God is still blessing him, his decision was a good one. Suddenly a fire burns down his entire building and all of his stock, and then he discovers that his accountant accidentally missed the last two payments on his insurance and it has been canceled. Of course, he becomes angry with the accountant and is even a little miffed at God because of this tragedy. He has to close his business because he doesn't have the money to rebuild, and even worse, he has to file bankruptcy because he owes creditors and has no money to pay them.

*What happened?* he wonders. *Things were going so well!* Then he remembers his decision to cut back on quality in order to make more profit, and he also remembers his lack of peace about doing it— and that he did it anyway. This man opened a door for Satan to bring destruction into his life through blatantly disobeying God. Don't let greed cause you to become dishonest in any way, because the person who walks in integrity will be blessed.

> *Don't let greed cause you to become dishonest.*

## Being Honest

Being honest is part of what it means to walk in integrity. Proverbs has much to say about the importance of being honest.

An honest witness tells the truth, but a false witness tells lies.

> Proverbs 12:17

The Lord detests lying lips, but he delights in people who are trustworthy.

> Proverbs 12:22

We should never cheat anyone. After shopping, if we get home and find we were not charged for an item, we should go back to the store or call and make arrangements to pay for it. We should not charge more for an item than it is worth. We should give eight hours of work for eight hours of pay. If you go to work and spend two hours of your day on personal phone calls or placing orders for personal items on the Internet, it is stealing. Does this sound harsh? All you need to do is ask yourself: If I were the employer, would I want my employees doing that?

When we are dishonest, it weighs on our conscience, even though we may have gotten very good at ignoring the whispers that something isn't right. When we do the right thing, we feel light and free, but doing the wrong thing on purpose leaves us with a heavy heart and, quite often, the fear of being found out.

The Bible teaches us to keep our word even if doing so is personally painful to us (Psalm 15:4).

Paul encouraged those he taught to be honest with one another, and to be truthful at all times (Ephesians 4:25). Truth is vital to being able to trust. We trust God because we know that He always keeps His Word; it is impossible for Him to lie (Hebrews 6:18), and we should be the same way.

Having integrity with our word is an area that deserves serious thought, because we can fall into the habit of saying whatever we need to say to avoid trouble. For example, you might be asked why you were late for work and quickly say, "Traffic was heavy due to an accident," but the truth is that you left your house too late because you spent too long on a phone call you should have not made before leaving for work. Telling the truth is important for many reasons, but one of them is that it forces you to face the truth. If asked why you were late for work and you say, "I made a phone call I should not have made, and I got out of the house late," you then have to face truth instead of avoiding it. This helps you not to keep making the same mistakes over and over. Jesus says the truth makes us free (John 8:32).

Being honest is about much more than not robbing a bank or a market. Most of you who are reading this book would not even consider doing something like that. However, you might take ten sugar packets home with you every time you eat in a restaurant, or you may take office supplies home for personal use. Why? Because many people see these infractions as minor. They don't think they matter, but they do. Not being honest, even in small matters, prevents us from being authentic, and it displeases God.

## Say What You'll Do, and Do What You Say

People seem to find it very easy these days to say they will do something and then simply not do it, without any explanation or communication. I find this very disturbing, because it seems to me that keeping our word is a basic and foundational principle by which we should live. God always keeps His word, and since we represent Him in our daily lives, we should follow His example. When Jesus said, "Follow Me" to His disciples, He didn't merely mean to follow Him around physically, but to watch and imitate

His behavior. He wanted them to watch how He handled people and situations, and then do as He had done.

The purpose of studying God's Word is to get to know Him and to be transformed into His image, learning to behave as He did. God's Word is very important, and there is no disagreement between what He says and what He does. The same should be true of us.

Jesus is the most authentic person who ever lived. He came to represent His Father God and to

> *Jesus is the most authentic person who ever lived.*

show the world what He was like. Now He wants us to do the same for Him. We are ambassadors for Christ.

When we tell someone we will do something, we have made a commitment, and we should always follow through and keep our word unless doing so is absolutely impossible. When that happens, we should communicate with the person we committed to and be honest about why we cannot do as we said we would.

## Saying Words You Don't Mean

I think most of us are guilty of trying to impress people by saying things that we really don't mean. One time I had been ministering at a church, and Dave and I had become friendly with one of their assistant pastors and his wife. We spent quite a bit of time together during my visit. When we were ready to leave, without even thinking about what I was saying, or considering whether or not I was willing to follow through on it, I said, "You and your family should come to St. Louis [where we live] and spend a few days with us. We'll show you the city. We have the St. Louis Arch, Forest Park, a great zoo, an art and history museum, a science center, and great places to eat. I think you would really enjoy it if you came."

A few months later, I received a phone call from the assistant pastor I had invited to St. Louis. "We're ready to come," he said enthusiastically. I asked where he was going, to which he responded, "We are taking you up on your invitation to come and visit you. We can stay a week." I thought, *Oh no, I can't have company right now. I don't want them to come.* I told him I would call him back after I checked my schedule. As soon as I hung up the phone I started praying, asking God to get me out of the situation. I said, "Lord, what am I going to do?" He, of course, impressed upon me that I should keep my word, have them come, and spend the week with them—and that maybe this situation would help me learn to think before I speak.

I had issued the invitation so the pastor and his wife would think we really liked them and were nice people. But I didn't really want them to come spend a week with us. In the moment I invited them, I doubted they ever would visit us. This transpired in an instant of time, and I didn't even fully realize what I had done. But just as the Lord said, I did learn a lesson that has helped me ever since. I now know that when I say I will do something, God expects me to do it, and He expects the same from you.

There was a time when a person's word meant everything. If someone said, "You have my word that I will do it," that was all that was needed. But a person's word doesn't seem to be so valuable now. Now we need long, laborious contracts and multiple signatures that are notarized and witnessed.

The psalmist David wrote, "As for me, I will walk in my integrity" (Psalm 26:11 NKJV). I think the key words in this verse are *I will*. David was making a declaration and a firm decision to walk in integrity. This is something we must make a decision to do, because if we don't, it becomes easy to get caught up in today's moral downhill slide or to follow the bad example of others around us.

Giving our word is equivalent to making a vow, and Ecclesiastes 5:2–7 informs us that God destroys the work of our hands when we do not keep our vows.

## Called to Be Excellent

As Christians, we are called to be people of excellence (1 Peter 2:9; 2 Peter 1:3). When we are excellent, we exceed the requirements, go above and beyond what is normal, do more than enough, and do what is superior.

Doing what we do with excellence is another foundational principle of our ministry. God strongly impressed upon us in the early days to do whatever we did with excellence. This doesn't mean perfection or extravagance, but it means doing the best you can with what you have. You may be driving

> God doesn't bless sloppiness or laziness, but He does bless excellence and integrity.

a car that is twenty years old, but you can still keep it clean and serviced. Maybe you have not been able to purchase new clothes for a long time, but you can take good care of what you do have. God doesn't bless sloppiness or laziness, but He does bless excellence and integrity.

Isaiah 12:5 states that God has done excellent things, and we are created in His image, so we should also do what we do with excellence. Let us choose to be excellent people. Daniel had an excellent spirit (Daniel 5:12 AMPC), and he was promoted (Daniel 6:3). People of excellence and integrity are not mediocre; they are not average. They follow their hearts. They are not moved by the crowd or influenced by rejection, the fear of man, or anything else. They follow God and set an example for others.

Philippians 1:9–11 teaches us that we should choose what is excellent, abounding in love and "being filled with the fruits of righteousness" (NKJV). Are you willing to make a commitment to excellence? We do not serve an average God, and we should imitate Him. He is El Shaddai, the God of more than enough. To be mediocre means to be halfway between failure and success. That is not where I want to be, and I'm sure you don't want to be there, either.

Jesus says that we should go the extra mile (Matthew 5:41). Always remember to do your best, even or especially when no one is watching you, knowing that God is always watching. Do it to glorify Him. Let me encourage you to do everything you do with all of your heart, knowing that God is watching, and so is the world.

Anytime we do less than what we know to be the best, we lose a little of our authenticity. Above all else, let us be real and genuine. Always do what you say you will do, be honest in every way, tell the truth, walk in integrity, and be excellent.

# PART 3

# Moving Forward as the Real You

# CHAPTER 18

# Pure in Heart

*Blessed are the pure in heart, for they will see God.*

Matthew 5:8

People who are pure in heart are powerful. *Pure in heart* is another way of saying authentic. When people are pure in heart, their outer life is consistent with their inner life. They are not pretenders. They do what they do with right motives. For example, they don't pray in public in order for people to see and admire them. They don't give generously to be well thought of or applauded. They don't help people in need and then feel that the ones they helped owe them something in return. Those who are pure in heart do what they do because they sincerely believe it is what God wants them to do. A person may be pure in heart and still make mistakes, but that is because they have weaknesses that have not been corrected yet. They are quick to repent once they see their error. Their desire is always to please God and help people, and they are happy to learn anything about themselves that will help them do so.

What did Jesus mean when He said that the pure in heart would see God? Did He mean they would see God in person, or was He implying something else? I think He was talking about blessings such as these: They would hear from God more clearly, experience the joy of His presence, and recognize His leading and guidance. We won't see God with our eyes until we get to heaven, but we can see the effects of His work in the earth and in nature, and we can sense His presence and guidance.

The Message version of Matthew 5:8 says, "You're blessed when you get your inside world—your mind and heart—put right. Then you can see God in the outside world."

The pure in heart will find faith to carry them through every situation and into a place of victory. When the heart is not pure, faith is hindered. Leonardo da Vinci was a famous painter, and children visited him often. When a child accidentally knocked over his canvas when he was trying to paint a picture of Jesus, he became very angry and ran off all of the children. He discovered he couldn't paint the face of Jesus until the hindrance of anger was removed.

> When the heart is not pure, faith is hindered.

Consider these hindrances that can block our faith:

- Negative emotions such as anger, self-pity, or jealousy
- Unforgiveness, bitterness, or resentment
- Offense
- Critical judgment toward others
- Murmuring, complaining, grumbling, or faultfinding
- Hidden sin that you fear will be discovered and for which you have not repented
- Fear
- Bitterness toward God because you feel your life has been unfair or your prayers have not been answered

Faith is a spiritual force, and it can only be released when our heart doesn't accuse us of wrongdoing before God. In order for us to walk in faith, trusting God to meet our needs, we must have confidence in God and believe that He loves and accepts us. However, if we know that sin is in our heart, it weakens us. Then, no matter how many excuses we make, we still sense a distance or a hindrance between God and ourselves.

We may fool people, but God knows the truth. The only way for us to find freedom is to face the truth and come into agreement with God's desires for us. Agreeing with God's Word, no matter what we think, feel, or want, is the wisest thing to do. God is always right, and it is useless to disagree with Him. During my early years of serving God, I can recall occasions when Dave and I argued. Quite often, after we finished arguing, I would sense God guiding me to apologize to Dave, but I didn't always do it right away because I thought that wasn't fair. It seemed to me that I apologized to Dave most of the time, but he rarely, if ever, apologized to me. I eventually learned that it was not my place to question God but to promptly obey, trusting that His ways are always best no matter how they seem to me.

> *God is always right, and it is useless to disagree with Him.*

God's Word teaches us to forgive and bless our enemies and those who have treated us cruelly. What could seem more unreasonable and unfair than that? However, if we do it, then God can become our Vindicator, and He will reward us for our obedience to Him. People who are pure in heart want to do God's will once they know what He wants them to do.

## How to Really Know Yourself

If we can truly know ourselves, I believe we are well on our way to developing a pure heart. The way to know oneself is to face the truth according to God's Word and to compare our behavior to it. Jesus says:

> If you hold to my teaching, you are really my disciples. Then you will know the truth, and the truth will set you free.
>
> John 8:31–32

To hold to His teaching could mean to adhere to it or to be diligent to do it. The obvious inference in John 8:31–32 is that if we know and obey the truth, it will set us free. Free from what? Free from the misery that arises from living in sin.

Facing truth about ourselves may be one of the most difficult things we can do. Many people spend a lifetime blaming others for their mistakes and wrong behavior, making excuses for them, and overlooking them. When they are confronted with the truth and realize they must take responsibility for their actions, they are shocked. This is difficult and wonderful at the same time. It is difficult because they are accustomed to their old ways, and now they must change; it is wonderful because nothing is better than living before God with a pure heart.

God desires truth in the inner being (Psalm 51:6 AMPC), so let us all learn to be truthful with ourselves. King David made this statement about God desiring truth in the inner being while he was dealing with the reality of his sin with Bathsheba. He had committed adultery with her. When she became pregnant, he had her husband, a loyal warrior in David's army, killed in battle. David had done these terrible deeds, yet for about a year, he ignored his sin and did not repent until the prophet Nathan confronted him (2 Samuel 12:7–9). His prayer of repentance, which you can read in Psalm 51, is quite moving.

Although David committed reprehensible acts, God still referred to him as a man after His "own heart" (1 Samuel 13:14; Acts 13:22). This was confusing to me until I learned that weakness is different than wickedness. David had a weakness concerning Bathsheba, and it caused him to do awful things, but he also loved God and truly had a heart that wanted to follow Him. I am so glad that God sees beyond our actions. He doesn't see as human beings see; He looks at the heart (1 Samuel 16:7).

## Hidden Sin

Hidden sin keeps us trapped, but bringing sin out into the light destroys its hold on us. God's Word teaches us to confess our faults to one another so we can be healed and restored spiritually.

> Hidden sin keeps us trapped, but bringing sin out into the light destroys its hold on us.

Confess to one another therefore your faults (your slips, your false steps, your offenses, your sins) and pray [also] for one another, that you may be healed and restored [to a spiritual tone of mind and heart]. The earnest (heartfelt, continued) prayer of a righteous man makes tremendous power available [dynamic in its working].

James 5:16 AMPC

Proverbs 28:13 teaches us that people who try to conceal their sin will not prosper. God's Word brings light, and that light shines on and reveals any darkness in a person's life. We should welcome the light and love it. According to Psalm 85:10 (NKJV), mercy and truth meet together, meaning that anytime we face truth, God's mercy is available to forgive and cleanse us from our sin.

## Listen to Yourself

One of the best ways to know yourself is to listen to the words you speak. Consider what Jesus and various Old and New Testament writers had to say about this:

- Jesus says, "The mouth speaks what the heart is full of" (Matthew 12:34).
- Jeremiah writes, "The heart is deceitful above all things and beyond cure" (Jeremiah 17:9).
- James observes, "Those who consider themselves religious and yet do not keep a tight rein on their tongues deceive themselves, and their religion is worthless" (James 1:26). Apparently, deceiving ourselves is very easy to do, and we need to pray sincerely that God will show us truth, so we won't live in deception while thinking we are just fine.
- Obadiah states, "The pride of your heart has deceived you" (Obadiah 3).
- Paul warns us, "Do not think of yourself more highly than you ought" (Romans 12:3).
- Peter says, "Humble yourselves, therefore, under God's mighty hand, that he may lift you up in due time" (1 Peter 5:6). Pride, in this instance, would be to go our own way no matter what God's Word teaches. Humility, on the other hand, would be to do what God's Word teaches no matter what we think, feel, or want.

How can listening to yourself help you? Let's start with a simple example and say you are in a situation that tempts you to be jealous of a friend. To figure out whether you really are jealous, simply ask yourself, "What comes out of my mouth when I hear about or see someone blessed in a way I have not been blessed? Am I truly happy for that person, or do I mutter, 'It must be nice to have everything handed to you in life!'?"

Do you ask a lot of questions to compare yourself with others, hoping to feel that you are better than they are? For example, do you ask people, "How much do you weigh?" "How much money do you make?" "How long do you pray each day?" "How much of the Bible have you read?" "How much did your dress cost?" "What's your educational background?" Questions such as these usually come from insecure people who feel good about themselves only if they feel superior to others.

Do you want to know if you are truly a positive person? Then listen to how much you do or don't complain. We can locate ourselves by listening to ourselves.

> *We can locate ourselves by listening to ourselves.*

Ask yourself also what your conversation reveals about you when you face difficult times in your life. Do you remain thankful, speak of God's goodness, and continue helping others? Or do you murmur and complain about your situation and feel that you are not being treated fairly by people or perhaps even God?

And for all the women who are reading this book, I wonder: What do we say when we see a very attractive woman? Do we say, "She is a beautiful lady," or "She probably had a face-lift, a tummy tuck, and liposuction; wears a wig and false eyelashes; and may be bulimic"?

I once had a very good friend who, anytime God used anyone to bless me with something special, said, "I'm waiting for someone to do things like that for me, too." She did care about me, but her comments let me know that she was jealous and envious of what I had been given. I eventually stopped telling her when God blessed me in special ways because her comments made me sad and uncomfortable.

You can help yourself grow and mature by simply letting your words expose what is in your heart. Once you know what's in your heart, you can ask God to help you deal with it effectively so you can become more like Him.

## Believing the Best

To the pure [in heart and conscience] all things are pure, but to the defiled and corrupt and unbelieving nothing is pure; their very minds and consciences are defiled and polluted.

Titus 1:15 AMPC

When people have a pure heart, they believe the best of others instead of being negative, suspicious, critical, and judgmental. Sometimes, those who have been hurt struggle to trust other people. Their inclination is to be suspicious, because they think it will protect them from being hurt again. They may have said to themselves over and over, "You can't trust anybody," and that thought is so embedded in their minds that they automatically conclude that anything even remotely suspicious is negative.

We once had a trusted employee of many years steal from the ministry offerings. This was shocking to us, but the person who had suspected him had proof that could not be refuted. His excuse was that he intended to pay it back. This is a good example of how people make excuses for behavior they know is wrong in order to ease their guilty conscience. Because I had known this man for many years and was so stunned by his behavior, I found myself thinking, *I will never trust anyone again.* However, God quickly reminded me that adopting that attitude would not be fair to other people. Love always believes the best of everyone, according to the apostle Paul's teaching on love in 1 Corinthians 13:4–7.

When someone is rude to us or hurts our feelings, we can avoid being offended if we choose to believe they didn't do it on purpose—because, most likely, they didn't. Recently someone called my attention to the fact that I had failed to compliment or show gratitude to someone who had done something for me. They quickly followed with, "I know you are grateful and didn't mean to hurt anyone." I appreciated their confidence in me, and although it was hard to hear, I was glad in the end that it was brought to my attention, because the last thing I want to do is hurt someone's feelings or be ungrateful. I didn't mean to be ungrateful, and I was very glad that the people involved were willing to believe the best of me.

Paul wrote to Timothy:

> The object and purpose of our instruction and charge is love, which springs from a pure heart and a good (clear) conscience and sincere (unfeigned) faith.
>
> 1 Timothy 1:5 AMPC

The word *unfeigned* means sincere, genuine, and without hypocrisy. Unfeigned faith is authentic faith, and we can see that to be authentic one must be pure in heart. We are called to walk in love above all else, and in order for that love to be sincere, we must be pure in heart.

## Why Did You Do That?

*Why* we do what we do is more important to God than *what* we do. He wants us to have pure motives (reasons) for our actions.

> Why *we do what we do* *is more important to God* *than* what we do.

Anytime I teach on the subject of motives, the room usually becomes very quiet, because people have to think. We are usually in such a hurry in life going from one thing to another that we rarely ask ourselves, "Why am I doing this?" However, this is a question we should ask, because God's Word makes it clear that our motives are very important to Him.

First Corinthians 3:13–15 says that when we stand before God on Judgment Day, our work will be shown for what it is because it will be brought to light. It will be revealed with fire, which I believe to be the eyes of Jesus, and that fire will test the quality of each person's work.

If what we have done survives the fire, we will receive a reward. But if it is burned up, the person will suffer the loss of their reward, but they will be saved. This affirms that we are not saved because of any work we have done, but we do receive or lose rewards based on the purity of our works.

The Bible teaches us in multiple places that when we go to heaven, we will receive rewards based on the works we have done. Those rewards are not merely based on what we have done but on why we have done it. Jesus says that if we do good works to be seen or to be well thought of, we "will have no reward" (Matthew 6:1).

The apostle John told his readers to "watch" themselves so they wouldn't lose what they had worked for, "but may win a full reward" (2 John 1:8 ESV).

To have a pure heart is, in essence, the same as having pure motives. I encourage you to take time to think not only about what you are doing but also about why you're doing it. This helps you not to lose rewards and will also help you avoid doing things merely to please people when those actions do not reflect God's will for you. Your peace and joy will increase since you won't be at war within yourself because you are doing one thing while believing you should be doing something else. Unity within one's own life is important, and it produces energy that enables you to live life with passion and zeal.

# CHAPTER 19

# Your Inner Life

*I know of nothing more valuable, when it comes to the all-important virtue of authenticity, than simply being who you are.*

Charles Swindoll

We should be more concerned with our inner life than we are with our outer life. The apostle Peter communicates this idea well:

> Your beauty should not come from outward adornment, such as elaborate hairstyles and the wearing of gold jewelry or fine clothes. Rather, it should be that of your inner self, the unfading beauty of a gentle and quiet spirit, which is of great worth in God's sight.
>
> 1 Peter 3:3–4

This clearly teaches us that God is more concerned with who we are on the inside than with who we are on the outside. What's inside of you is the real you.

> We should be more concerned with our inner life than we are with our outer life.

People may be impressed with how we dress, our jewelry, our hairstyle, our neighborhood, the car we drive, and many other things about us, but none of those external trappings shows who we really are. Someone can be rich in possessions yet very poor in soul and spirit (the inner life). We can dress up, go out, have lunch with three people, and spend the afternoon telling them how great we think they are and how much we admire them, all while thinking about how much we dislike them and how boring we think they are. Why do people behave this way? Because they want to impress people or gain something from them.

> Is your reputation on earth more important to you than your reputation in heaven?

We earn our reputation with people through the way we live our outer life, but our reputation with God is based on the way we live our inner life. Let me ask you: Is your reputation on earth more important to you than your reputation in heaven? I hope not. No matter how much we pretend to be something or someone we're not during our earthly lives, the day will come when all things will be exposed for what they are. Jesus teaches us to beware of hypocrisy, saying, "There is nothing concealed that will not be disclosed, or hidden that will not be made known. What you have said in the dark will be heard in the daylight, and what you have whispered in the ear in the inner rooms will be proclaimed from the roofs" (Luke 12:2–3).

## Looking Good

Most of us want to be sure that we look nice before we leave our homes and venture out in public. I spend a lot of time getting ready, especially if I am going to a place where a lot of people will see me. I have to take a shower and wash my hair, then blow-dry my hair and style it with a flat iron. I don't have the kind of hair that can be washed and styled once a week; mine has to be done every day. I've tried to tell Dave how blessed he is to be a man, because he requires so little time to get ready to go anywhere compared to the time it takes me. He reminds me that he has to shave, and women don't have to shave, and then I remind him that I have to put on three or four kinds of skin cream and then put on makeup—and we all know how precise that needs to be. Then I need to pick out just the right outfit, and sometimes that requires trying on a few of them to make sure I have the right one. Then I need to select the right shoes, because we know the shoes make the outfit. In addition, we have to accessorize the entire thing with just the right jewelry and maybe a scarf. Sometimes preparing to leave the house is quite an ordeal. Since this will eventually be shouted from the rooftops, I may as well admit that I am probably a little vain. (The Lord and I are still working on that one.)

Thankfully, though, God has taught me to make sure my insides are well prepared for the day before I start on my outsides. I get up in the morning and head for the coffee pot and Jesus (they make a good team). I spend time with the Lord first thing every day and remind myself that my reputation with Him is much more important than how I look or what I possess. I urge you to make it more important to keep your inner life even more attractive than your outer life. We can dress ourselves up and go to church and perhaps impress a few people along the way, but God sees the hidden person of the heart, and that is what He wants to be beautiful.

I can remember years when Dave and I argued all the way to church, perhaps yelling at the children for making too much noise in the back seat of the car. But as soon as we arrived and started seeing people, our entire demeanor changed, and we became a perfectly loving family. As I say, we quickly got out and put on our "church faces."

All of us have many different faces—masks that we wear and change, depending on where we are going. Perhaps you have one mask for your church friends and a totally different one for your work friends. If so, that is definitely not authentic. In Jesus' day, pretenders and hypocrites heard some stern words from Him (Matthew 23:13–36), and those same words apply to us if we are not authentic.

## Inner Purity = Outer Power

In a sense, we have two lives—a natural life and a spiritual life. Both should come under the guidance and leadership of the Holy Spirit. We don't have to work on both, because if we are living in obedience to God in the inner life (mind, will, emotions, conscience), we will live in obedience to God in the natural life. If we pretend to live for God in our natural, daily life while our inner life is far from Him, we gain nothing. God is not pleased with such pretension.

God's Word helps us understand the inner and the outer life. Paul says that even though our outer person is "wasting away," our inner being is "renewed day by day" (2 Corinthians 4:16). The prophet Habakkuk said that while we have all kinds of trouble in our outer natural life, we are making spiritual progress as we "rejoice in the Lord" (Habakkuk 3:17–19). This is because choosing to do what we believe God wants us to do even while enduring personal difficulty causes us to grow and mature spiritually. According to Revelation 3:17 and 2:9, people can think they are rich and yet be poor, and they can look poor and yet be rich. Let me say again that what we have inwardly is more important than what we have outwardly.

A person may not have many possessions yet be rich in godly

character, knowledge of God, fellowship with God, and faith in Him. Likewise, people may look at all of their possessions and beautiful outfits and think they are rich, yet they are poor if they don't know God, have ungodly character, or are filled with the ugliness of hatred, jealousy, anger, pride, or other qualities God disapproves of. My life changed dramatically once I learned to make my inner life a priority and realized it was much more important than how I look or what I own. We impress no one if God is not pleased with us.

## The Kingdom of God

As we read and study God's Word, we frequently come across the phrase *the kingdom of God*, but what is God's kingdom? Simply put, a kingdom is a realm over which a king rules, so God's kingdom is the realm over which He rules and reigns. Jesus taught that the kingdom of God is within us (Luke 17:21). It is our inner life. It is the home of God and the realm where King Jesus should rule. Just imagine, according to Scripture, our inner life is the home of God, and I'm sure we want Him to be comfortable in His home in us.

> Don't you know that you yourselves are God's temple and that God's Spirit dwells in your midst?
>
> 1 Corinthians 3:16

What would make the Holy Spirit uncomfortable in our hearts? Anger, hatred, unforgiveness, jealousy, greed, critical and judgmental thoughts toward others, rebellion, stubbornness, and other attitudes the Bible warns us not to have. Anything that our Lord has commanded us not to do would make Him uncomfortable if He were living in the midst of it. We should honor His presence in us and make sure that what goes on in our inner life is pleasing to Him.

*We should honor God's presence in us and make sure that what goes on in our inner life is pleasing to Him.*

Remember that, according to God's Word, the Lord loves and delights in a heart (inner life) that is gentle and quiet (1 Peter 3:4). Have you ever focused on simply making sure that you remain calm on the inside at all times? Doing so would eliminate a lot of problems. One thing you would not do is worry about or fear the future. I am dealing with several situations right now that could easily cause me to worry, but remembering that God loves a quiet spirit helps me remain calm.

First Peter 3:4 states that a heart that "is not anxious or wrought up" (AMPC) is precious in God's sight. I suggest that you spend some time pondering how much of the time you are quiet and peaceful on the inside compared to how much time you are anxious or agitated. Be honest in your assessment, and if you need to make changes, ask God to help you. As you obey Him, He will guide you into peace.

## The Inner Dimension

The inner dimension is a busy place, and the Holy Spirit is like a traffic light that tells us whether to stop, go, or proceed with caution. We have a lot of self-talk going on all day (yes, we all talk to ourselves), and what we say is important. The term *self-talk* refers to our thoughts. We have imaginations, attitudes, motives, purposes, conscience, emotions, desires (will), and intuition (knowing or revelation). Hopefully, we also have an abundance of good fellowship with God, but it is possible for these other things to prevent us from having time for that.

One of the wisest, most important things we can do is realize how important the inner dimension is and take responsibility for what we allow to go on in it. Some people feel completely worn out because of what goes on inside of them. Inner turmoil (the opposite of quiet) causes sickness, nerve problems, unhappiness, discontentment, premature aging, behavior that is hard to get along with, and spiritual, mental, and physical weakness. Inner purity equals power, but inner turmoil and impure motives equal weakness.

> *Some people feel completely worn out because of what goes on inside of them.*

## Dedicate Your Inner Life to God

But the Lord said to him, Now you Pharisees cleanse the outside of the cup and of the plate, but inside you yourselves are full of greed and robbery and extortion and malice and wickedness.

You senseless (foolish, stupid) ones [acting without reflection or intelligence]! Did not He Who made the outside make the inside also?

But [dedicate your inner self and] give as donations to the poor of those things which are within [of inward righteousness] and behold, everything is purified and clean for you.

Luke 11:39–41 AMPC

Let me ask you to slowly reread the three verses above and reflect on what they are saying. Consider especially what it means to dedicate your inner life to God. When we dedicate ourselves to something, it means that we devote ourselves and our effort, time, and energy to a purpose or task. We cannot maintain inner purity unless it becomes a matter of importance to us and we focus on maintaining it.

We often run so hard and fast trying to make sure everything in our outer life looks good and is pleasing to other people that we may totally forget how important the inner life is. Perhaps we have never realized this in the first place. My prayer is that this information is an awakening for many of my readers and a reminder for others. Simply writing this book has made me more aware of my inner life, and I find myself paying more attention to what is going on inside of me.

As I alluded to in the previous paragraph, life has become complicated and challenging for most of us. We are pressured to multitask, hurry, and rush. The only way I have found to remain peaceful on the inside is to purposefully slow down and refuse to get sucked into a vacuum of pressure from the world. One way to do this is to become an expert at saying no when you need to. It is up to each of us to set boundaries to prevent people and the world's system (which Satan rules) from running our lives while we barely notice what is happening to us. Since almost everyone is stressed beyond reasonable limits, "stressed" has become the acceptable and even admired way to live. If we are not busy, we are made to feel that we have no worth or value—unless, of course, you know the truth, which is that your worth is not found in being busy but in loving God and knowing how much He loves you.

God created us for fellowship with Him. He wants a portion of our time and desires that we

*God created us for fellowship with Him.*

discuss our decisions with Him before we make them. Before God ever created humankind, He made the decision that He would sacrifice His only Son for our sins. God has never been surprised by our behavior. Cain didn't shock God when he killed Abel. David didn't shock God when he committed adultery with Bathsheba and had her husband killed to hide his sin. And God has never been shocked or surprised by my sins or yours. Just try to imagine how much God must want relationship with us, since He knew ahead of time that we would sin and that sacrificing His Son Jesus would be the only way to redeem us.

In addition, think of the fact that Jesus knew what He was being asked to do and agreed ahead of time to do it. The Bible states that the Lamb of God was slain before the foundation of the world (Revelation 13:8). God lives outside of time and space and knows the end from the beginning, so although He was fully aware of how the human race would turn out, He so strongly desired relationship with us that He was willing to sacrifice Jesus, His beloved Son, for our sins. I don't know about you, but this thought is astounding to me. Jesus suffered terribly on the cross as He was crucified, and He bore the punishment of the sins of everyone for all time. I can't even comprehend this with my finite mind. Surely, the least we can do is love Him and dedicate our inner lives to Him so we can create a home in which He can enjoy living. We are very blessed that God loves us so much.

CHAPTER 20

# Be Filled with the Holy Spirit

*The fulness of the Spirit is not a question of our getting more of the Holy Spirit, but rather of the Holy Spirit getting more of us.*

Oswald J. Smith

Have you ever tried to pour water into a bottle that was already full? Of course not! You know that would not work. You can only fill an empty container.

In order to be filled with the Holy Spirit, we need to be empty of ourselves. For now, I will simply say we need to be empty of self-centeredness or selfishness, but I will expand on the idea of emptying ourselves later in this chapter. I often say that I was not filled with the Holy Spirit until I finally came to the end of myself—the end of my strength, the end of my reasoning, the end of my human efforts and abilities. Only when we reach the end of ourselves are we ready to be filled, for as long as we are self-willed, we can't be filled with God's will. As Oswald J. Smith said in this chapter's opening quote, it is not a matter of our "getting more of the Holy Spirit, but rather of the Holy Spirit getting more of us." All believers have the Holy Spirit dwelling in them, but having something is different than being

> In order to be filled with the Holy Spirit, we need to be empty of ourselves.

filled with it. The Holy Spirit deeply desires to occupy any part of us that we are willing to give Him, and anytime we give Him access to an aspect of our being, it makes our lives easier and more fruitful.

Let me ask you: Are you full of God or full of yourself? Paul wrote to the Ephesians and prayed they would be filled through all their being and "become a body wholly filled and flooded with God Himself" (Ephesians 3:19 AMPC). This is a clear and concise statement. God's Word teaches us to "ever be filled and stimulated with the [Holy] Spirit" (Ephesians 5:18 AMPC).

Here is a simple way to look at what happens to us when we receive Jesus as our Savior and the work the Holy Spirit needs to do after that: When we are born again, we receive Jesus and His Holy Spirit into our human spirit, but He also desires to occupy our soul (our mind, will, and emotions). This is accomplished as we cooperate with the work of the Holy Spirit as He matures us.

Spiritual maturity is necessary for those who desire authenticity and want to embrace their uniqueness. We can say without a doubt that Jesus was authentic, and He was definitely unique. He always said what He meant and meant what He said.

> Spiritual maturity is necessary for those who desire authenticity and want to embrace their uniqueness.

When we are born again, we are in the baby stage of Christianity, but as all parents want for their children, our Father God wants us to mature and grow up spiritually. This takes place over a period of time, or as Paul put it, we are transformed into Jesus' image "with ever-increasing glory" (2 Corinthians 3:18) as we look into His Word:

And the Lord—who is the Spirit—makes us more and more like him as we are changed into his glorious image.

2 Corinthians 3:18 NLT

Notice that 2 Corinthians 3:18 says this change comes from the Lord, who is the Spirit. It comes from Him, and it cannot be done without Him, but we must be willing to let Him do the work He needs to do in us. Since we have free will, God does not force us to do anything. He guides, but we must be willing to follow.

Philippians 2 describes very clearly the work that needs to be done in us:

Therefore, my dear ones, as you have always obeyed [my suggestions], so now, not only [with the enthusiasm you would show] in my presence but much more because I am absent, work out (cultivate, carry out to the goal, and fully complete) your own salvation with reverence and awe and trembling (self-distrust, with serious caution, tenderness of conscience, watchfulness against temptation, timidly shrinking from whatever might offend God and discredit the name of Christ).

[Not in your own strength] for it is God Who is all the while effectually at work in you [energizing and creating in you the power and desire], both to will and to work for His good pleasure and satisfaction and delight.

Philippians 2:12–13 AMPC

This passage is one of the best scriptural descriptions I know of to explain the work that needs to be done in us. Although the Holy Spirit does the work, we are also to work it out to the full, but not in our own strength. Here again, I take this to be an instruction for us to work with the Holy Spirit during our growth process.

Our mind must be renewed, our emotions must be controlled, and our will must choose God's will rather than its own way. We are all very attached to what we think, how we feel, and what we want—and we don't give it up easily. Thankfully, God is patient, and He continues to work with us, convincing us to submit willingly to His ways.

It is important for the world to see Jesus through us, and that can only happen to the degree that the Holy Spirit occupies our soul. Have you surrendered to God? If not, are you willing to do so now? Is there any area in your life that you are holding back from Him? If so, then it is an area that He will not fill.

> Have you surrendered to God?

We usually need to start with the renewing of the mind, meaning that we learn to think according to God's Word instead of accepting and taking as our own any random thought that comes to our mind. To know the difference, we must know God's Word. The more we think as God thinks, the more of His goodness we will experience in our lives (Romans 12:2).

Our mind is connected to our emotions and to our will, so as we learn to think like God does, our emotions and will are also changed.

## Spirit—Soul—Body

We are spirit beings, we have a soul, and we live in a body. At death, we leave our body, but the spirit and soul live forever, and we get a new glorified body. I'm really excited about that, because there will be no pain, no cellulite, and no getting tired or feeling bad. We will spend eternity in heaven if we have believed in and received Jesus Christ as the sacrifice and payment for our sins, and we will spend eternity in hell if we have rejected Him.

Many people are uncomfortable with talk about hell, and in more recent times some so-called scholars have tried to entirely remove the doctrine of hell from Christian teaching. I see no reason for the mention of hell making us uncomfortable if we are living as God wants us to live. I've heard people say they don't believe in hell because no loving God would send anyone there, and they are right. God doesn't send people to hell; people make their own choice regarding where they will spend eternity according to how they live their life on earth.

*Sheol* (an Old Testament word) is translated *hell* thirty-one times, *the grave* thirty-one times, and *the pit* three times. The Greek word *Hades*, which is translated *hell*, is mentioned ten times in the King James Version of the New Testament. Jesus talked about hell more than any person in the Bible, and He actually spoke of hell more than He spoke of heaven. He also described hell in greater detail than He described heaven. Any research on hell leaves us with no doubt that it will be a most unpleasant place. Choosing where we want to spend eternity should not be difficult.

I personally think a little more teaching on hell would be helpful. We rarely hear sermons that include this topic, yet Jesus spoke of it frequently. People need to remain aware that the choices they make now will affect where they spend eternity.

While we live on Earth, God wants to work through our soul and our body. We are ambassadors for Christ, and He is making His

*Other people cannot see that we are saved unless they see our salvation in our behavior toward them.*

appeal to the world through us (2 Corinthians 5:20). Other people cannot see that we are saved unless they see our salvation in our behavior toward them and the way we live in this world.

When Jesus began His public ministry, John the Baptist, the forerunner to Jesus who was called to prepare His way, said, "He must increase, but I must decrease" (John 3:30 NKJV). It was time for John to slip into the background and bring Jesus forward. Perhaps it is time for some of us to slip into the background, so to speak, and let Jesus come forward.

I believe authentic Christians want spiritual maturity and are willing to do whatever the Holy Spirit guides them to do to gain it. They cannot be satisfied to learn and never practice what they have learned. If they don't live it out in their daily lives, all they have is head knowledge that puffs them up with pride instead of a living experience of knowing Jesus in their daily lives.

## Inner Healing

You may have heard the term *inner healing* and wondered what it meant. It refers to the healing of a wounded soul. I wrote a book titled *Healing the Soul of a Woman*, and it has been very popular. Many people are hurting inside. Their emotions are wounded from past hurts, and they don't think in ways that benefit them. Instead, they are usually tormented by negative, fearful, insecure thinking and by bitter thoughts toward those who hurt them. Their will is damaged, so they don't make good choices. They are often rebellious toward any kind of authority, and when they don't get what they want, they rarely respond graciously. They need inner healing, and Jesus can and wants to give it to them. Because they have been hurt, they feel the world owes them something, yet they often try to collect from people who had nothing to do with their original wounding. After having been sexually abused by my father and abandoned by my first husband, I found myself in the early years of my marriage to Dave trying to collect from him what I felt I was owed. He could not repay me, though, because only God could give me what I needed—a sense of being loved, valued, precious, secure, confident, and at rest in my soul.

During those painful years, I did not understand any of what I understand now. I reacted to every situation out of wounded emotions and was completely filled with myself. Jesus says that if we intend to be His disciples, we need to forget ourselves and take up our cross and follow Him (Mark 8:34). Our "cross" is not to bear tragedy, loss, disease, or lack, but to live unselfishly.

> Our "cross" is not to bear tragedy, loss, disease, or lack, but to live unselfishly.

Jesus "died for all, that those who live should no longer live for themselves but for him" (2 Corinthians 5:15). Yes, Jesus died to save us from our sins, but He also died to free us from ourselves. We can and should surrender our lives to Him and live for what He wants.

To put this in the simplest terms possible, I think we can say that most people just want to be happy, and a person cannot be selfish and happy at the same time. Jesus calls the selfish life "the lower...life," and a life lived for Him "the higher...life" (Mark 8:35 AMPC).

Until the wounded soul is healed and made whole, we find being unselfish impossible. One reason for this is that we are so fearful of being hurt again that we feel the need to protect and take care of ourselves.

> Until the wounded soul is healed and made whole, we find being unselfish impossible.

As we study God's Word and spend time with Him, He renews our mind, heals our emotions, and teaches us to submit joyfully to Him, because His love makes us feel safe.

## The Problem of Self

With our spirit, we contact God; with our body, we contact the world; and with our soul, we contact ourselves. Since we desire to be filled with God's Spirit and know that only an empty container can be filled, let me suggest some of the "self" problems we need to recognize and deal with so we will no longer be filled with them. I have come across all of these terms multiple times over the years and cobbled together definitions that I think explain them well:

- *Selfish:* Concerned mainly for oneself without regard for others
- *Self-analysis:* Being excessively introspective or obsessive about analyzing one's behavior, mistakes, or flaws
- *Self-conscious:* Excessively or uncomfortably aware of one's appearance or manner
- *Self-critical:* Severely judging one's own faults
- *Self-righteous:* Doing right and good to feel right about oneself; this causes the judgment of others
- *Self-justifying:* Makes excuses for faults when being corrected
- *Self-sufficient:* Independent, providing for self without asking for help
- *Self-indulgent:* Excessive gratification of one's desires
- *Self-will:* Obstinate, gratifying one's own self
- *Self-abasement:* Degradation due to feeling inferior
- *Self-pity:* Feeling that one is being treated unfairly; becomes self-idolatry because the person's mind is only on themselves

These are just several words that show us how prevalent self-focus is. If you were to search for "self" words in a dictionary or on the Internet, the list would seem endless. Yet Jesus calls us to live selfless lives, thinking not about ourselves but about others. To take up our cross—to live unselfishly, in order to be Jesus' disciple (Luke 9:23)—is a task too big for any human to tackle alone. So, the first "self" issue to deal with is self-sufficiency. Admit that you can't live an unselfish life in your own strength, and ask God to work in and through you until selfishness is replaced with the same kind of love that God shows through Christ.

Learning to live selflessly is not a onetime event, but a process that will unfold over time as you walk with God. You may begin by dealing with self-sufficiency, but all of us also have other areas of self-focus we must also deal with and overcome with God's help. Each part of your soul that you are willing to release to God is an aspect of your life that can be filled with His Spirit.

# CHAPTER 21

# Enter God's Rest and Be Yourself

*Our rest lies in looking to the Lord, not to ourselves.*

Watchman Nee

It is impossible to be authentic or to be your unique self unless you learn how to rest in the Lord. Otherwise, you will constantly be striving to try to be what you think everyone else wants you to be. You will labor to try to change yourself into someone you admire, rather than resting in God and believing that He created you and that all you can ever be is yourself. Trying to be someone else is frustrating, because you are trying to do something you can never do. John Grisham says, "Don't compromise yourself—you're all you have."

Entering God's rest is not about sitting in a chair or lying on a bed; it is about learning how to rest internally. We can lie in bed and worry all night, and that is not rest. The body may be resting, but the soul is working, working, working. This is why some people never feel rested, no matter how much sleep they get. Jesus says that if we will come to Him when we are weary, He will give us rest for our souls:

Come to me, all you who are weary and burdened, and I will give you rest. Take my yoke upon you and learn from

me, for I am gentle and humble in heart, and you will find
rest for your souls.

Matthew 11:28–29

Notice that He said for our *souls*. When our soul is at rest, we
are confident in Christ, and we trust Him to help us do whatever we need to do. We know that
He accepts us and that we need
not worry about those who might
reject us. We are free to be who
we are—our own authentic and
unique selves.

> When our soul is at rest, we are confident in Christ, and we trust Him to help us do whatever we need to do.

After God finished creating the world, He looked at everything
He had made and said that it was good—and that includes you
(Genesis 1:31). You may not be like anyone else, but you are a
beautiful person. Everyone else in the world may see it, but if you
don't see and accept it, you will continually strive to be something
you can never be.

When you think about yourself or look in the mirror each day,
know that God wants you to be able to rest in the way He has created you. When He designed and crafted you, He created someone beautiful. He wants you to think of yourself as "good" and
beautiful, because that's the way He sees you. He also wants you
to accept yourself, because He loves you and accepts you just as
you are.

## Rest Is Not Inactivity

Resting in God does not mean inactivity. It is not a rest *from* work,
but a rest *in* work. When I step onto a platform and face several

thousand people who have come hoping I will say something that will answer their questions, encourage them, and teach them, I could feel a lot of pressure, but thankfully, I don't. I did at one time, but God has now taught me how to rest in Him. Without that, the stress would have been too much for me.

Before I learned to rest in God, I was self-conscious about how I looked. *Am I dressed all right?* I would ask myself. *Do the people like me? Am I being too aggressive or straightforward? Do I have the right message?*

I jumped between faith and doubt during the entire event. If anyone looked at their watch, I was sure they were bored and couldn't wait until the session was over. If anyone left early, I was sure it was because they didn't like me or my message. When I finished, I was exhausted physically, mentally, and emotionally, but it wasn't from the physical work I had done; it was because I lacked confidence in Christ. I worried while I worked, and it left me worn out. When I went back to my hotel room, I worried more about the message I had taught. I wondered if it had been the right one, and I thought excessively about any mistake I thought I had made. I tried so hard to be just right and do everything just right, but all that did was torment me. I could not hear God when He was saying, "I created you and guided you as you asked Me to, and it was good," because I was operating in fear instead of faith.

> I worried while I worked, and it left me worn out.

I finally did learn to rest in God while I work for Him. Without that lesson, I doubt that I would still be in ministry. The stress would have caused some kind of health problems that would have prevented me from finishing what God wants me to do, or I would have given up because of the sheer agony in my soul.

As you learn to rest in God while you work, remember that

God thinks you are beautiful. He looks at you and says you are "good." Maybe no one in your life has ever noticed the good in you, affirmed you, or assured you of your unique beauty and value. Perhaps people have viewed the special qualities about you as negative in some way, while God views them as very good. If so, your Father, God, will undo any damage that unkind opinions or comments have done to your soul. He will teach you to be confident and to understand that something unique has more value than something with a thousand copies. Each of us is hand-crafted by the Almighty, and He doesn't make mistakes.

Let me ask you: Can you look in the mirror and say, "God has made me special, and I am beautiful to Him?" Or, when you have prayed and asked for God's help with the job you are doing, can you hear Him say, "It is good!"? I challenge you right now to believe that when God created you, He created something good.

## Be Yourself or Be Defeated

First Samuel 17 tells the story of David and Goliath. The Israelite army faced a huge giant named Goliath, a champion of the mighty Philistines. However, when Goliath came forth to fight, the Israelite soldiers were terrified and refused to answer Goliath's challenge to fight him (1 Samuel 17:1–11, 16).

David's father, Jesse, had sent him to the battle in order to take food to his brothers, who were watching. While David was there, Goliath came forward again, and the men of Israel fled in terror before the giant (2 Samuel 17:12–24). While the warriors of Israel were terrified of this giant, David said, "Who is this uncircumcised Philistine that he should defy the armies of the living God?" (1 Samuel 17:26). David felt that it was a disgrace for the Israelites to flee from this giant. As he began asking questions, his brothers

grew angry with him. His oldest brother belittled him by reminding him that he was only a shepherd who tended to a few sheep
and asking him why he had come to the battle (1 Samuel 17:28).

David's father thought he was sending him to feed his brothers,
but God had a much greater plan in mind. This story reminds
me that God always has you right
where you need to be, at just the
right time, and to get you there,
He will use people who don't even
know what they are doing.

> God always has you right
> where you need to be, at just
> the right time.

David's reply to his brothers shows that he was accustomed to
their unkind treatment. "'Now what have I done?' said David.
'Can't I even speak?'" (1 Samuel 17:29). David turned away from
them and began asking questions of others who were there. This
was brought to the attention of King Saul (1 Samuel 7:30–31).

David offered to go and fight the giant, but King Saul immediately told him no, because he was too young and the giant
had been a warrior for many years. David then immediately
recounted a time when he had slain a lion and another when he
had slain a bear, apparently with his bare hands (1 Samuel 17:32–
37). Finally, Saul agreed to let him fight. Then he dressed David
in his own tunic and armor and put a bronze helmet on his head.
David walked around a little and then told Saul that he couldn't
go fight dressed in his armor, because he wasn't accustomed to
it. He took off Saul's armor, took a staff in his hand, and gathered
five smooth stones and a slingshot. Armed with only those items,
he approached the giant (1 Samuel 17:37–40).

Goliath made fun of David because he was only a young boy
and began to threaten and taunt him with the harm that he
intended to do to him (1 Samuel 17:41–44). But David replied,
"You come against me with sword and spear and javelin, but I

come against you in the name of the Lord Almighty, the God of the armies of Israel, whom you have defied" (1 Samuel 17:45). Young David went on to tell the giant what he would do to him in that name. David did defeat Goliath (1 Samuel 17:46–51), but he had to be himself in order to do so. His ways may have been unorthodox, but they worked because God was with him.

Always remember that you cannot defeat your Goliath with Saul's armor on, meaning that you cannot use someone else's abilities, personality, or resources to accomplish what you need to do. Learning to be yourself is essential for any kind of victory in your life. The world may not understand your uniqueness, but God does, and that is all that matters.

# CHAPTER 22

# Be Real

*Always be a first-rate version of yourself, instead of a second-rate version of somebody else.*

Judy Garland

In a biological sense, every person has life—a breathing existence in which they live day after day. But many are discontented, searching for something more than they experience each day, yet not knowing what they are searching for. They want to know what their purpose is and why they are on earth.

The Bible reveals a different quality of life that is available to us in Jesus Christ. He is the real life for which every person is searching. When we are born of God (born again) and receive Christ as Lord and Savior—the only sacrifice for our sins— we experience a new life, a real life, one in which we know we are born to enjoy, fellowship with, and serve God. In Him, we are content, complete, and fulfilled.

The apostle John writes at length about this life. He refers to Jesus as "the Word of life" (1 John 1:1). Several times John refers to those born of God (1 John 3:9; 4:7; 5:1, 4, 18). He was born of God; this experience was a reality to him, not something he inherited from someone else. He had personally encountered Jesus; he had touched Him physically but been affected spiritually. He traveled with Jesus, watched Him, and learned from Him.

This life that John speaks of goes far beyond something we read about; it is a life we experience. We know that Jesus lives. He is alive in us. We trust Him, and that trust makes Him real to us. He is our everything. As Paul writes, "In him we live and move and have our being" (Acts 17:28). This life is very different from the natural life with which we were born; it is a spiritual life. This is a life that was exciting to the apostle John and others who knew Jesus during His earthly ministry, and it can and should be exciting to us, too.

## The Counterfeit versus the Real

There are counterfeit Christians and real Christians, and we can learn to discern the difference. The United States government employs people whose job is to locate counterfeit money. They train for their job not by studying counterfeit money, but by studying the real money over and over until they are so well acquainted with the look, feel, smell, and details of real money that they can quickly recognize counterfeits.

Suppose you have a counterfeit ten-dollar bill that you think is genuine. You use it to pay for groceries, and the grocery store owner uses it to pay for supplies. Then the supply company takes it to the bank along with other money it is depositing, and the bank teller says that the bill is counterfeit. Along the way the ten-dollar bill did a lot of good, but it was eventually shown to be exactly what it was: a fake.

The same principle applies to counterfeit Christians. They may do good works, but when they face the final judgment, they will be rejected. Jesus spoke of those who would say to Him, "Lord, Lord, did we not prophesy in your name and in your name drive out demons and in your name perform many miracles?" To them

He will say, "I never knew you" (Matthew 7:22–23). I am sure they will be shocked. Now is the time for each of us to ask if we are real Christians or counterfeit Christians. Let's ask ourselves: Have I been truly born of God? Or do I merely attend church,

> *Now is the time for each of us to ask if we are real Christians or counterfeit Christians.*

do some good works, and have a Christian bumper sticker on my car and a few plaques around my house with well-known Scripture references on them?

How can we tell the difference between a real Christian and a counterfeit? Jesus says that we will know them by their fruit (Matthew 7:16, 20), meaning what their lives produce. A child of God lives a righteous life and does not practice sin. A true believer will occasionally commit sin, but he doesn't make a habit of it.

> No one born (begotten) of God [deliberately, knowingly, and habitually] practices sin, for God's nature abides in him [His principle of life, the divine sperm, remains permanently within him]; and he cannot practice sinning because he is born (begotten) of God.
>
> 1 John 3:9 AMPC

The next verse states, "By this it is made clear who take their nature from God and are His children and who take their nature from the devil and are his children" (1 John 3:10 AMPC). All we need to do is watch the fruit of people's lives. God's Word makes clear what is the fruit of the Holy Spirit and what is the fruit of the flesh (Galatians 5:16–23). For real Christians, the Lord Jesus is the center of everything. When we are born again, we are given the divine nature of God (2 Peter 1:4).

The real Christian has fellowship with God. People hate

loneliness, but those who are born again are never alone. True believers have joy, peace, and the righteousness of God in Christ (2 Corinthians 5:21; Romans 14:17). Real Christians walk in the light, not the darkness. They know their sins are forgiven, and they should be not burdened with guilt about past sin.

Being a real Christian does not mean that all of our days are perfect or that we are never sad. We face difficulty, trials, and tribulations, just as other people do, but we never face them alone, for God is always with us.

## Stay on Fire

Jesus says, "I know your [record of] works and what you are doing; you are neither cold nor hot. Would that you were cold or hot! So, because you are luke-warm and neither cold nor hot, I will spew you out of My mouth!" (Revelation 3:15–16 AMPC).

> We must remain active and not allow ourselves to become lazy and lukewarm.

Revelation 3:2 urges believers, "Wake up! Strengthen what remains and is about to die." This is an interesting scripture informing us that we must remain active and not allow ourselves to become lazy and lukewarm. Paul wrote to Timothy to "fan into flame the gift of God" (2 Timothy 1:6). He also wrote, "Never lag in zeal and in earnest endeavor; be aglow and burning with the Spirit, serving the Lord" (Romans 12:11 AMPC).

I learned a long time ago that nothing good happens acciden-tally. To be a real Christian with accompanying fruit, I will need to stay on fire for God and His purpose in my life. I cannot let myself become lazy or lukewarm. We don't do good works to earn salvation, for it is a gift of God's grace, which we receive

*Nothing good happens accidentally.*

through faith. We do good works *because* of our salvation, because of what God has done for us in Christ Jesus, and because we love Him. We do them because it is our new nature to do them.

## The Proof Is in the Fruit

The fruit of a counterfeit or immature Christian is evident in many ways. For example, counterfeit Christians say one thing and may even instruct others in certain ways, but they do something else themselves. They are hypocritical. They usually criticize others, gossip, and harbor unforgiveness toward those who have hurt them. They tend to be jealous, greedy, and self-centered. These are only some of the lusts of the flesh they may display. Real, spiritually mature Christians also sin and are certainly not perfect, but their lives are marked by sincere love,

*Always look for good fruit in people's lives.*

generosity, desire to help others, kindness, patience, and deep desire to grow spiritually and become more and more like Jesus.

Always look for good fruit in people's lives. What they produce is more important than what they say they are. It is easy to talk like a Christian, but the real proof is in the fruit. I recall being very hungry one day while I was driving somewhere, so I stopped at a grocery store and went in to purchase something to eat. I walked by the oranges, and they were large and sumptuous-looking, so I bought one. I paid one dollar for it, which was a high price at the time. I took the orange out to my car, placed a paper towel on my lap, and proceeded to peel the fruit. Everything was going just fine until I took my first bite, and I knew right away that the way that orange looked didn't properly represent how it would taste. When I squeezed it, there was absolutely no juice. It was dry and tasteless, but it looked beautiful.

I have learned that people who claim to be Christians may look good, but we never really know what's inside them until they are squeezed (put under pressure) or tasted (meaning that we have personal experience with them). Don't be overly impressed by the way people look, by what they say, or

> It is better to focus on walking in love than to focus on trying not to sin.

even how they seem to be upon initially meeting them. Be patient and make sure they are not counterfeit. Always search for the real thing when you think about those with whom you want to be involved, spend time, and be friends.

## Let Your Love Be Real

Paul writes that our love should be real, sincere, and without hypocrisy (Romans 12:9). True, sincere love must always be given in order to help or bless others. We must not merely pretend to be kind, while secretly wanting to put someone in our debt or to be hoping to be well thought of and admired.

Jesus says that loving God and loving others as we love ourselves are His new commands for us (Matthew 22:37–40; Mark 12:29–31). If we walked in perfect love, we would never sin against God or people, but only God can love perfectly. I think it is better to focus on walking in love than to focus on trying not to sin. I find that focusing on the positive, on what God wants me to do, will keep me from doing what He doesn't want me to do.

Think of it this way: If I were to go on a diet in order to lose some weight, I would be better off to think of all the good food I could eat rather than focusing on what I couldn't eat. Thinking of what I can't do makes me feel I am under the law and only makes me want to do those things more. If you told me I *had* to eat chocolate ten times a day, I would probably begin to hate chocolate, even though right now I enjoy it. We are meant to be free and led by the Holy Spirit rather than to live under rules and regulations.

> If we want to walk in love, we should focus on what we can do in order to be a blessing to others.

If we want to walk in love, we should focus on what we can do in order to be a blessing to others. Everyone wants to be encouraged, complimented, and told they are valuable. I have not run across anyone who doesn't like to receive a gift, especially if it is given for no reason except that I want to bless them.

One of the most shining facets of love is that it always forgives quickly. I think it is a good idea to examine our heart daily and ask ourselves if we have anything against anyone. If we do, we should forgive them, remembering how often God forgives us.

## How to Recognize Love

In 1 Corinthians 13, Paul teaches us how to recognize love by telling us what the fruit of love is:

> Love is patient, love is kind. It does not envy, it does not boast, it is not proud. It does not dishonor others, it is not self-seeking, it is not easily angered, it keeps no record of wrongs. Love does not delight in evil but rejoices with the truth. It always protects, always trusts, always hopes, always perseveres. Love never fails...And now these

three remain: faith, hope and love. But the greatest of
these is love.

(1 Corinthians 13:4–8, 13)

Just think about how much better life would be if we all
believed the best of one another. We would not be tormented by
suspicion and evil thoughts about other people. Believing the
best of others helps us even more than it helps them. It is a facet
of love that allows us to enter and enjoy God's rest. This is something I endeavor to practice, and I urge you to do likewise. Study
all the Bible verses you can find on loving others. I did a quick
check while writing this book and found one list containing one
hundred verses on loving others.
One of my favorites is 1 Peter 4:8:
"Above all, love each other deeply,
because love covers over a multitude
of sins."

> Believing the best of others helps us even more than it helps them.

I found another list of one hundred Bible verses about God's
love for us. You can find an abbreviated version of this list and
the one on loving others in the back of this book.

The only way we can love others is to receive God's love for
ourselves. Remind yourself daily of how much God loves you,
and let that love flow through you to other people. Although we
all like to hear the words *I love you*, love is more than "theory or
in speech"; we should love "in deed and in truth (in practice and
in sincerity)" (1 John 3:18 AMPC).

One time when I was seeking God about why walking in love
seems to be so difficult to do, He taught me that it is because
love always costs us something. It costs us time, money, or effort.
God's love for us was expensive. It cost Him the life of His Son.

Jesus suffered because He loves us, and if need be, we should be willing to suffer or be unselfish in order to show love to others. The world is filled with hurting, lonely people who are searching for unconditional love. When they don't have it, they fill that void with destructive pursuits that may feel good for a little while but are harmful in the end—things such as unhealthy relationships, substance abuse, gambling, and excessive spending for possessions they think will make them feel better about themselves. This is a sad reality for many people.

*Love always costs us something.*

God loves all people unconditionally, but real Christians may be the only ones through whom they can experience that love. Will you let God love someone through you? A counterfeit Christian may speak words of love, but the action is missing. When that happens, ultimately the person who needs love ends up more disappointed and disillusioned than ever before.

*Love is seen in how we treat people, not in how we feel about them.*

Love is much more than a feeling. Love is seen in how we treat people, not in how we feel about them. We can even show love to our enemies if we remember that God loved us "while we were still sinners" (Romans 5:8), and we can do the same for others.

When we take ministry trips to third-world countries or do outreach here in the United States to share the gospel with people, we always meet practical needs while we are there. We provide food, clothing, homes, clean water wells, medical care, and other benefits freely for all. We add the words "Jesus loves you, and so do we," but we let them feel the love through our actions.

Sometimes we must go back several times before they truly believe we will be consistent and do more than just talk about love, but love never fails.

Recently in an interview I was asked "When you are gone from the earth, Joyce, how do you want people to remember you?" I answered, "I want them to remember that I loved them with God's love."

> I want people to remember that I loved them with God's love.

If we focus on loving God and loving people, we will be happy. We will also bring joy to others and put a smile on God's face. Love is what the world needs, but it must be real and authentic, or it is useless.

# CHAPTER 23

# Be Confident

*This is the confidence we have in approaching God: that if
we ask anything according to his will, he hears us.*

1 John 5:14

I intentionally placed this chapter on confidence in the latter part
of this book because in order to be confident, we must believe
the things I have already written about—such as learning to love
yourself, understanding that failure is part of learning how to
succeed, recognizing the danger of being a people-pleaser, believing that you are unique, knowing that you must be authentic,
and realizing that you can be free from the fear of rejection.

True confidence doesn't begin with confidence in ourselves but
with confidence in God. Look again at the opening scripture of
this chapter and take a few moments to consider the impact of

> True confidence doesn't
> begin with confidence
> in ourselves but with
> confidence in God.

what it says. We can approach God
with confidence, knowing that He
hears us "if we ask anything according to his will," and if He hears us
He will grant our request at just the
right time.

And if (since) we [positively] know that He listens to us in
whatever we ask, we also know [with settled and absolute

knowledge] that we have [granted us as our present possessions] the requests made of Him.

1 John 5:15 AMPC

First John 5:15 offers us the most amazing invitation—to confidently interact with God in an intensely personal way. Note that the amplification says that our requests are "granted us as our present possessions," which means that we have them by faith. Faith is so real that asking and believing is the same as already having what we ask God to give us. God cares about everything that you care about. He is for you, and you can be confident that He will never leave you or forsake you (Hebrews 13:5). If we learn to do everything we do because we believe it is God's will, and we totally depend on Him for the grace (power) to be successful, we will be able to go through life confidently and without letting fear control us.

> *God cares about everything that you care about.*

We must have confidence in God before we can live our lives with confidence. He is our confidence. In his commentary on Hebrews titled *Be Confident*, Warren Wiersbe writes:

> The epistle to the Hebrews is a book we need today. It was written at a time when the ages were colliding and when everything in society seemed to be shaken. It was written to Christians who were wondering what was going on and what they could do about it. The stability of the old was passing away, and their faith was wavering.
>
> One of the major messages of Hebrews is *Be Confident!* God is shaking things so that you may learn to live by faith and not by sight. He wants you to build your life on

the permanence of the eternal and not on the instability
of the temporal.

I heard a story about a man who went to the doctor about his
hearing. Although he had worn a hearing aid for twenty years, he
had never been able to hear well. The doctor removed the hearing
aid from his ear, and immediately the man could hear better. For
twenty years, he had been wearing the hearing aid in the wrong
ear! Sometimes the message we hear is right, but our hearing
is wrong. Sometimes experiences from our past may affect our
understanding of what we hear.

> *We are often more interested in conquering a book than we are in truly understanding it.*

I also heard an anecdote about
a pastor who asked another pastor if he had a deaf ministry in his
church. The other pastor replied
that he often felt everyone in his
church was deaf, because they never seemed to hear what he said.

Sometimes we seem to be this way. We may hear but not really
listen, and we may read but not take the time to truly comprehend. We are often more interested in conquering a book than
we are in truly understanding it. I want to make sure you know
what a rare privilege it is to go before the throne of God boldly
and with confidence, talk to Him about anything that is on your
mind, and know that He cares and wants to help you. Surely that
one fact should give us the confidence to do anything else we
need to do in life.

Confidence is actually faith; it is a belief that we are capable of
doing something. We are wise to never forget that we are capable
only with God's help and by His grace, and that without Him we
can do nothing (John 15:5). As long as our confidence is in God,
we will continue enjoying success in our ventures. Paul instructs

us to have "no confidence in the flesh," but only in Christ Jesus (Philippians 3:3). As soon as I put my confidence in my own ability, God will have to let me fail in order to bring me back to confidence in Him alone. The flesh—our carnal nature—loves credit, but it is very important that we do not take the credit that belongs to God alone.

> As long as our confidence is in God, we will continue enjoying success in our ventures.

## We Need Confidence

If we have little or no confidence, we won't even come close to reaching our potential in life. As children of God, we have so much available to us that we will never even ask God for unless we have confidence that He loves us and delights in our prayers. Paul encourages us to come to the throne and ask "fearlessly and confidently and boldly" for God's help (Hebrews 4:16 AMPC). James 4:2 says that we do not have certain things because we do not ask for them. God is able to do "superabundantly, far over and above all that we [dare] ask or think" (Ephesians 3:20 AMPC), so we should never be satisfied with a little, because God can do a lot. Be content where you are, and enjoy

> We should never be satisfied with a little, because God can do a lot.

where you are, but never stop wanting to grow and give God more and more glory through the work you do for Him.

Let me encourage you to dream big dreams, even ones that seem impossible, because all things are possible with God (Mark 10:27)! Confidence is our spiritual right; it is part of our inheritance as joint heirs with Jesus Christ. You can be assured that "no weapon forged against you will prevail, and you will refute every

> Confidence is part of our inheritance as joint heirs with Jesus Christ.

tongue that accuses you. This is the heritage of the servants of the Lord" (Isaiah 54:17). The Amplified Bible, Classic Edition translation of this scripture states that "peace, righteousness, security, triumph over opposition" are our heritage from the Lord.

We must be secure in God's love and secure in our own uniqueness if we want to be confident. Insecurity is rampant in our society today; it is a psychological problem of epidemic proportion. People who search for security in all the wrong places always end up disappointed. However, if we look to God for our security and keep Him as our first priority, we will enjoy security in our everyday lives and situations. If we know that God is with us, guiding us and upholding us, we will have the freedom to live life confidently.

If I had something to lift that weighs one hundred pounds, it would be too heavy for me to lift alone, so I would not be confident that I could do it. But if Dave said he would help me lift the load, then I could approach the weight with confidence. I would know that when I had done what I could do, Dave would take over and lift it the rest of the way. In life, we need to let God do the heavy lifting.

When we lack confidence, it causes all kinds of other problems. Fear dominates us and prevents us from doing what we truly desire to do. True joy escapes us because "fear involves torment" (1 John 4:18 NKJV). I believe any lack of confidence grieves the Holy Spirit, because it prevents Him from doing through us what He desires to do. We lose our individuality and end up being a counterfeit of someone else. If we don't believe we are acceptable, we find someone who we think is what we should be, and we try to emulate them in a desperate attempt to find acceptance for ourselves also.

Confidence protects us from other torments that Satan wants

> Any lack of confidence grieves the Holy Spirit, because it prevents Him from doing through us what He desires to do.

to bring into our lives, such as self-hatred, condemnation, perfectionism, seeking the approval of people in unbalanced and unhealthy ways, and allowing others to manipulate and control us. A lack of confidence makes you feel inferior, but as Eleanor Roosevelt said, "No one can make you feel inferior without your consent." If you lack confidence, begin working to change your beliefs about yourself. Being positive about yourself is easier than being negative. Believe that God loves you and that you are special, and return to this truth as often as possible. Trust that He has given you abilities that are unique and that you are an unrepeatable, one-of-a-kind child of God.

You don't have to *feel* confident to *be* confident. Live and behave in a confident way, no matter how you feel. As you begin to practice living out of a belief in your worth, strength, and abilities, your feelings will soon catch up with your decision to be confident in every situation. I believe most people's primary problem in life is that they allow their feelings to control them instead of living beyond feelings and making decisions according to the truth of God's Word.

## Individual Uniqueness

When a man and woman marry, they are said to become one, but that doesn't mean that they give up their individuality. Dave and I are uniquely different from each other. We don't have the same strengths or weaknesses. Where I am weak, he is strong, and where he is weak, I am strong. So we complete each other and can function as one whole.

When Paul speaks of believers, he compares our roles in God's kingdom to one body with many different parts. All parts of the body are necessary, although some are not as visible as others (Romans 12:4–5; 1 Corinthians 12:12–27). When we become jealous of another person's position due to lack of confidence and insecurity, we make ourselves miserable trying to be something we are not and never can be.

## Relax and Be Yourself

God determines our temperament while we are still in our mother's womb. When children are very small, you can begin to see each child's unique, individual temperament. Your children may have the same parents, but they are each uniquely different from one another.

When God called Joshua to replace Moses after Moses' death and told him to take the Israelites into the Promised Land, he said something that I love.

> No one will be able to stand against you all the days of your life. As I was with Moses, so I will be with you; I will never leave you nor forsake you.
>
> Joshua 1:5

*When God is with us, it doesn't matter what we lack because He will be our strength in weakness.*

God didn't tell Joshua that he had to try to be like Moses. He said, "As I was with Moses, so I will be with you." You see, when God is with us, it doesn't matter what we lack because He will be our strength in weakness. Taking the place of someone like Moses would have been a daunting task, and the pressure would have been crushing had Joshua not understood that he could relax and be himself rather than trying to be like Moses was. When you find yourself in a new and challenging situation, try to let go of your desire to control and instead depend on God, because if He is with you, nothing else matters.

Confidence is one of the most beautiful qualities in the world. It is contagious, but so is a lack of confidence. If you have confidence, people will follow you. Your con-

> No matter how much others believe in you, if you don't believe in you, then you have failed before you even try.

fidence gives them confidence. But no matter how much others believe in you, if you don't believe in you, then you have failed before you even try.

You can believe in yourself because God believes in you. When Gideon was busy being a coward and talking negatively about himself, God called him a mighty warrior (Judges 6:12). If we could only see ourselves as God does, then we could relax and let God do mighty things with and through us. Don't ever try to be more than what you are, but don't try to be less than what you are, either. Be determined to reach your full potential for the glory of God.

Moses was like Gideon in that he initially argued with God about his capabilities. Moses was certain that God had the wrong man. He told God he couldn't speak eloquently, that he was slow of speech and awkward (Moses is believed to have stuttered). God told him, "I will be with your mouth and will teach you what you shall say" (Exodus 4:12 AMPC). Moses told God that the people would not believe him, but God said, "I will be with you." (Exodus 3:12). Moses talked so much about his inabilities that God finally grew angry and told him to speak to Aaron and that Aaron would speak for him.

God used plenty of people who did not feel their natural abilities qualified for what He called them to do, but when they found in Him the confidence to step out in faith, they did great and mighty things, and so will you.

I need to say that we want to be confident but not conceited or proud. It is important that we don't even sound arrogant to others, and we can avoid doing so simply by the way we talk. My confidence is in Christ, and I trust Him to work through me. I am only confident because I know that He loves me and is with me all the time. Always be sure when conversing with other people that you give God the credit that is due Him. Corrie ten Boom, a Dutch woman who helped many Jews escape the Nazis in World War II and was a survivor of Ravensbrück camp herself, received compliments all the time when she later became a public speaker. She said that she gathered each compliment as you would gather flowers in a bouquet, and at the end of the day, she gave the entire bouquet of praise to the Lord. The more Jesus does through us, the more thanksgiving and praise we should offer Him.

Be bold, be strong, be confident, and let God amaze the world through you!

# CHAPTER 24

# Be Comfortable with God

*Mental prayer is nothing else...but being on terms of friendship with God, frequently conversing with Him in secret.*

Teresa of Avila

Is it possible, or even right, to have a comfortable friendship with God? Some would quickly say no. They tend to think that reverential fear, awe, and worship of such a mighty one as God eliminates the possibility of such comfortable thoughts as being His friend. But God's Word teaches us that being comfortable with Him and relating to Him as a friend is not only possible but proper.

> Being comfortable with God and relating to Him as a friend is not only possible but proper.

We are, of course, to have great reverence for God and to be in awe of Him, always realizing that He is omniscient (knows everything), omnipotent (has all power), and omnipresent (is everywhere all the time). We should always be respectful, being careful not to offend Him, but we are also invited into friendship with Him. Although He sits on His throne in heaven, He is not far away because His Holy Spirit lives in us. We serve one God who manifests in three persons—God the Father, God the Son, and God the Holy Spirit. Sadly, the Holy Spirit often gets the least attention, but it should not be that way. He is the one whom Jesus sent after His death, resurrection, and ascension to represent Him and take His place. Jesus says that He lives in us. You can't get much closer than that.

> But the Comforter (Counselor, Helper, Intercessor, Advocate, Strengthener, Standby), the Holy Spirit, Whom the Father will send in My name [in My place, to represent Me and act on My behalf], He will teach you all things. And He will cause you to recall (will remind you of, bring to your remembrance) everything I have told you.
>
> John 14:26 AMPC

> The Spirit of Truth, Whom the world cannot receive (welcome, take to its heart), because it does not see Him or know and recognize Him. But you know and recognize Him, for He lives with you [constantly] and will be in you.
>
> John 14:17 AMPC

The Bible says that Abraham believed God, and it was credited to Him as righteousness (Genesis 15:6), and the apostle James refers to Abraham as "God's friend" (James 2:23).

If we want to be called a friend of God, we need to understand that, through Jesus at the new birth, we are made the righteousness of God in Christ (2 Corinthians 5:21). I mentioned this in an earlier chapter, but let me state again that being made righteous means that Jesus takes all our sin and gives us His right standing with God. This righteousness is available to us not because all of our actions are right, but because of God's gift of grace, so that we can draw near to God and develop a close relationship with Him.

Just as Abraham believed God and that belief was counted as righteousness, we also receive the righteousness of God through our faith if we believe in Jesus as our Lord and Savior.

Unless believers come to understand and accept by faith this right standing as our position with God, we will never enjoy the inheritance and liberties that belong to us as children of God.

Jesus told His disciples that He no longer called them servants "because a servant does not know his master's business," but He called them "friends" because He made known to them everything that He learned from His Father (John 15:15). Jesus shared important and intimate truths with them, things that His Father had told Him. Sharing is what happens between friends.

God wants us to draw near to Him, and He promises to draw near to us (James 4:8). The biggest change in my Christian life came when I learned that I could have an intimate, close friendship with God, rather than a stiff, formal one in which I had to try hard to be and sound religious when attempting to talk with Him. Before I learned that I could relax and be comfortable in God's presence, I was less than authentic because I tried to change who I really was in order to converse with and impress Him. The Lord wants us to come to Him as we are, without pretending to be a phony version of ourselves. He wants us to be authentic.

> *The Lord wants us to come to Him as we are, without pretending to be a phony version of ourselves.*

Seeing yourself as a friend of God is in no way disrespectful to Him, as long as you know in your heart that without Jesus you are nothing (John 15:5). Yet, through Him, we are blessed with every blessing from heaven that can be given to people in Christ (Ephesians 1:3). When we approach the Father in Jesus' name, we present to Him all that Jesus is, not what we are. Being a friend of God does not mean that we are on an equal level with Him. He is above all, in all, and through all (Romans 11:36). All things consist and are maintained by Him (Colossians 1:17; Hebrews 1:3).

We are to have the greatest amount of respect for God, but that does not mean that we cannot also be friends with Him. Friends share their lives with one another, they are comfortable together, they do things for one another, and they trust and enjoy each other. Madame Jeanne Guyon, a quietist who lived in France during the 1600s and 1700s, was very close to God and she said that enjoying God should be the goal of every Christian.

## God Is Not Mad at You

I spent many years living with the underlying fear that God was angry with me. I didn't even know what He was angry about, but I was sure I had made some mistake that disqualified me from ever being comfortable with Him or receiving His love and acceptance. This fear also left me with a vague feeling of guilt, even though I didn't always know what I felt guilty about. Feelings such as these are lies from Satan. I had believed them, and they gave me a completely wrong perception of God and left a gap between us, a gap I tried to bridge with good works. I had yet to learn that Jesus stands in the gap between us and God, and we are able to go to God through Him and be comfortable doing so.

As you have read, I grew up with an angry father, and I'm sure that was the root of my fear. Regardless of its origin, the fear I experienced throughout my younger years was tormenting. I loved the Lord and tried to live what I thought was a good Christian life, but my sins and mistakes—real or imagined—were ever before me, accusing me and leaving me feeling guilty, like a person on the outside of my life looking in. Not only was I not comfortable with God, but I didn't think being comfortable with Him would be doctrinally correct. Even though I had been born again, I still saw myself as a poor, miserable sinner. I didn't understand that I had a new identity in Christ and that although I did still sin, God saw me through Jesus' sacrifice and received me in Christ as He would Christ Himself.

I'd love to be able to tell you that this truth came to me quickly, but it took many years before I was willing to even dare to believe it. I pray it doesn't take you that long. If you have received Jesus as your Savior, know that God is not mad at you. He may not approve of everything you do, but He does approve of you as His child. As a repentant believer, I urge you to begin saying to yourself, "God is not mad at me! I am completely forgiven of all my sin and washed clean in the blood of Jesus." Meditating on these truths and confessing them verbally will help you build a new image of yourself, one that God wants you to have. If anyone is in Christ Jesus, they are a new creation altogether (2 Corinthians 5:17).

I am happy to report that now I rarely, if ever, feel guilty, because I know it is not God's will. Paul, inspired by the Holy Spirit, wrote that he wanted to do what was right but always ended up doing what was wrong (Romans 7:14–23). After he asked who would deliver him from this wretched condition, he then stated, "Thanks be to God, who delivers me through Jesus Christ our Lord!" (Romans 7:24–25).

He went on to say, "Therefore, there is now no condemnation for those who are in Christ Jesus" (Romans 8:1). The Bible is filled with such good news, and if we read it and believe, we cannot be anything but joy-filled.

## Why Is Righteousness So Hard to Understand?

I think the fact that we have been given the righteousness of God is hard to understand because we have spent so many years identifying with being a sinner. Even as born-again children of God, we have been told repeatedly that we are sinners. Indeed, we do sin, but it is possible to be regular attendees at a church and never hear that after receiving Jesus, He views us as righteous because of our faith, just as Abraham was. A search on the Internet revealed 106 New Testament Bible verses about sin and 106 about righteousness. Considering this, I wonder, why is so much emphasis placed on sin and so little on righteousness?

> *Why is so much emphasis placed on sin and so little on righteousness?*

Unless we understand the God kind of righteousness—the righteousness He offers us—we will never feel the liberty to become a close, intimate friend of God. How could we possibly approach such a Holy God without fear unless we understand that right standing with God has been imputed (assigned) to us as a gift? There's no way we can pay for it.

There are two kinds of righteousness. One is self-righteousness earned through our good works. God never accepts this kind of righteousness as adequate to make us right with Him. The other kind of righteousness is the one I'm writing about—the righteousness that only comes through faith in Jesus. This is the only kind of righteousness that is acceptable to God.

The devil does not want us to understand our right standing with God through our faith in Jesus. He wants to keep us feeling weak and useless, like sinners who always must cower before the throne of God begging for forgiveness. This picture is very different from the one presented in Hebrews.

For we do not have a high priest who is unable to empathize with our weaknesses, but we have one who has been tempted in every way, just as we are—yet he did not sin. Let us then approach God's throne of grace with confidence, so that we may receive mercy and find grace to help us in our time of need.

Hebrews 4:15–16

Jesus came to earth and took on human flesh so He could identify with us and be able to understand and sympathize with what we experience. He invites us to come to the throne of grace with confidence and receive forgiveness and mercy. That sounds much better than approaching with cowardice, being fearful that God is angry with us.

> *Jesus came to earth and took on human flesh so He could identify with us and be able to understand and sympathize with what we experience.*

## Righteousness and Prayer

Satan does not want us to understand our righteousness, because when a righteous person prays, tremendous power is available (James 5:16). Prayer is one of our greatest privileges. It is an honor, not an obligation. Just think about the amazing wonder of prayer. We, as born-again men and women, may go to God boldly and ask for anything with the confidence that God will grant our request if we have prayed according to His will (1 John 5:14).

> *When a righteous person prays, tremendous power is available.*

The Holy Spirit shows us how to pray as we should pray,

because He knows God's will (Romans 8:26–27). He helps us in our weaknesses and strengthens us to go to God with confidence, expecting Him to do even more than we have asked. Of course, Satan does not want us to pray, because in doing so we become partners with God, allowing Him to use us in the earth to accomplish His will. Satan wants us to be feeble, weak, fearful, and useless, but we can resist him in Jesus' name, and when we do, he must flee (James 4:7).

## Righteousness and Right Behavior

In chapter 7, I mentioned that believing we are made the righteousness of God will lead us to right behavior, but I want to say a little more about this because it is so important.

We can struggle all of our lives, trying in our own strength to do what is right, and we will continually fail unless we first receive God's righteousness by faith. If righteousness is in us because we have received it from God, we will demonstrate it through godly behavior.

Our behavior will never be perfect as long as we are in our flesh-and-bone bodies, but it will improve little by little all the time. We have a promise that He who began a good work in us will bring it to completion (Philippians 1:6). When we sin, all we need to do is admit it and repent (be willing to go in a new and right direction), and there is no condemnation. Immediately, we have a fresh start and we don't have to look back.

Change comes as a result of abiding in Jesus, not through struggle and self-effort. A fruit bush or tree abides and produces fruit on its branches in due time. The Holy Spirit is in us, and the fruit of the Spirit is in us (Galatians 5:22–23). As we rest (abide) in the knowledge of who we are in Christ, fruit (good behavior) will

manifest as a result. The more time
we spend with Jesus, the more we
will become like Him.

> Change comes as a result of abiding in Jesus, not through struggle and self-effort.

Always look at your progress in
becoming more like Jesus instead
of focusing only on how far you still have to go. Through the grace
of God, my behavior is so much better than it was when I began
my walk with Him. I still have a long way to go, but it doesn't
matter how far I have to go as long as I am making progress.
The same applies to you. Focus on your progress, and that will
produce more progress. Actually, I encourage you not to focus
too much on your faults or your progress, because doing either
keeps you self-focused instead of God-focused. All the glory for
any progress in our lives goes to God, and any future progress
that is needed only comes through dependence upon and obedience to Him.

When I have a weakness or fault that needs to be changed, I
begin by repenting and asking God to change me. Then I study
God's Word repeatedly in the area in which I need help, and I rest
in God, trusting Him to do what needs to be done in me.

## Righteousness and Joy

Right standing with God by faith produces peace and joy, and
joy leads to enjoyment. We all want to enjoy our lives, and God
wants us to enjoy them. Jesus said that He came that we might
"have and enjoy life, and have it in abundance (to the full, till it
overflows)" (John 10:10 AMPC).

Therefore, since we are justified (acquitted, declared
righteous, and given a right standing with God) through

faith, let us [grasp the fact that we] have [the peace of reconciliation to hold and to enjoy] peace with God through our Lord Jesus Christ (the Messiah, the Anointed One).

Through Him also we have [our] access (entrance, introduction) by faith into this grace (state of God's favor) in which we [firmly and safely] stand. And let us rejoice and exult in our hope of experiencing and enjoying the glory of God.

Moreover [let us also be full of joy now!] let us exult and triumph in our troubles and rejoice in our sufferings, knowing that pressure and affliction and hardship produce patient and unswerving endurance.

Romans 5:1–3 AMPC

Righteousness comes through faith, not through keeping rules. It is available to all who have faith, without distinction. Friendship with God is not something reserved for super Christians or some kind of specialized believer; it is available to everyone. The Holy Spirit is in you. He wants you to talk to Him, and He wants to talk to you. He often speaks through our own thoughts and helps us recognize that He is speaking.

*The Holy Spirit will speak to you in many ways.*

The Holy Spirit will speak to you in many ways. The more experience you have with Him, the more you will learn. We all make mistakes as we learn to hear God's voice, but it is foolish to deprive yourself of this benefit just because you may not get it right every time.

Let me encourage you to start talking to God all the time about everything that is going on in your life and all that is in your heart. Ask Him to teach you to hear from Him. Be authentically and uniquely you when you interact with God. Your conversations with Him will usher in a closeness and intimacy that you will greatly enjoy. Tell Him often throughout the day that you love Him, and be open to doing anything He may want to lead you to do. Don't let your relationship with God be reduced to an hour on Sunday morning or to a short morning and evening prayer. He wants to be involved in your entire life, because He loves you, enjoys you, and wants you to enjoy your relationship with Him.

> *Be authentically and uniquely you when you interact with God.*

# CHAPTER 25

# Believe

*Whoever believes in him is not condemned, but whoever does not believe stands condemned already because they have not believed in the name of God's one and only Son.*

John 3:18

I pray that through the reading of this book you have come to understand that being your authentic and unique self is very important. God loves you unconditionally and accepts you totally, and you should not try to perform or pretend for anyone in order to gain their approval or acceptance.

I have shared many truths with you in these chapters, but one thing remains, and only you can do it. It is to *believe*. Jesus says that if we only believe we will see His glory—the manifestation of His most excellent works (John 11:40).

> God loves you unconditionally and accepts you totally.

If we believe what God promises in His Word, our lives will be amazingly wonderful. That does not mean they will be without challenges or trouble, but our worst day with Jesus will be better than our best day without Him. He is with us in trouble and has promised to never leave or forsake us (Psalm 46:1; Hebrews 13:5). All things are possible with Him, and He gives us strength and

the ability to do whatever we need
to do in life (Mark 10:27; Philippians 4:13).

> *Our worst day with Jesus will be better than our best day without Him.*

If you ever feel your peace and
joy are missing, check your believ-
ing (Romans 15:13). Believing God makes life simple. We no longer have to struggle trying to find the why behind what we don't
understand. We can trust (believe) God and know that He will
reveal to us what we need to know when we need to know it.

You have read this book once, but I wonder what might happen if you read it again *with the specific purpose of believing what it
says?* We should not believe everything we read, because some of
it may be false information, but a book like this, which is based
entirely on God's Word, can and should be believed. I have provided ample Scripture references to give you an opportunity to
check out anything I have written, and I encourage you to do so.

To help you remember some of the lessons of this book, let me
ask you some questions about what you have read:

- Do you believe that God loves you unconditionally?
- Do you believe that you are acceptable to God?
- Do you believe that God wants you to be your authentic and
  unique self?
- Do you believe that you should live to please people or to
  please God?
- Do you believe that God is not mad at you?
- Do you believe that your sins are forgiven and the guilt has
  been removed?
- Do you believe that your self-image affects the quality of
  your life?

- Do you believe that God wants you to love yourself?
- Are you willing to take a step of faith and be your unique self, even if it means losing some friends?
- Are you willing to do what you believe God wants you to do, even if it means that other people may judge you critically?
- Do you believe that God has a wonderful future planned for you?
- Do you believe that you can let go of your past and move forward in life?

I encourage you to return to these questions as you allow the truth of God's perfect love for you to transform the way that you live day to day. Reading a book merely for the sake of conquering yet another book will not help you at all, except to make you proud that you have read another book. However, reading it and receiving the truth found in it for yourself *will* help you and change you for the better.

## It Will Be Done for You as You Believe

What we believe is powerful, because we will end up having or experiencing what we believe. Don't rush past this point; it is a good place to ask yourself what you believe. A centurion went to Jesus, asking Him to heal his servant. Jesus said to him, "Go! Let it be done just as you believed it would" (Matthew 8:13). On another occasion, two blind men followed Jesus and asked to be healed. Jesus said, "Do you believe that I am able to do this?" When they replied, "Yes, Lord," Jesus "touched their eyes and said, 'According to your faith let it be done to you'" (Matthew 9:28–29).

I want to mention again the importance of being authentic with God. If you struggle to believe, be truthful with the Lord about it.

Don't pretend to have faith you don't have. In Mark 9, we read about a father who comes to Jesus, asking Him to heal his son because a demon had tormented him since he was a child. The man said, "If you can do anything, take pity on us and help us" (Mark 9:22). Jesus says that all things are possible with God for those who believe. The father exclaimed, "I do believe; help me overcome my unbelief!" (Mark 9:24). The boy was healed and made whole.

I love the father's honesty in this story. He didn't pretend to have faith he did not have. I think we can all relate to this father. At times, we come to God and ask Him to do something. We do believe, but our faith is not perfect. We also have some doubt, some unbelief. I don't think anyone has perfect faith without ever experiencing doubt, but our faith becomes stronger and more perfected each time we use the faith we do have and see God work.

In these gospel accounts, we see instant results, but that is not always the case. Many times we ask, we receive by faith, and then we wait for God to act. Sometimes it is a short time, and sometimes it is a long time. The timing is up to God; our part is to continue believing.

When I am waiting for God to do something I have asked Him to do and I start to think about how long it has been, I say, "I believe that God is working on this situation right now, and I will see results in due time." First Thessalonians 2:13 confirms this:

And we also thank God continually because, when you received the word of God, which you heard from us, you accepted it not as a human word, but as it actually is, the word of God, which is indeed at work in you who believe.

As long as we continue believing, God continues working. God wants us to live "from faith to faith" (Romans 1:17 NKJV). But the

> As long as we continue believing, God continues working.

devil wants to continually inter-rupt our believing with doubt. We can say no to doubt and hold on to faith.

## Make a Decision to Believe

Believing is much easier than not believing. It is easier to be posi-tive (believe) than to be negative (not believe). Just this morning I was thinking about something I needed to do, and I started to worry about whether or not I could do it. I recognized what I was doing and decided to believe that when the time came, God would enable me just as He has so many other times in the past. You can make a decision to believe. You can replace all fear and worry with faith and confidence in God's promises. God has given us more than five thousand promises in His Word, and all He asks us to do is believe what He

> You can replace all fear and worry with faith and confidence in God's promises.

says. We have a tendency to believe only what we can see, but in God's kingdom we must believe first in order to ever see in real-ity. How can we do this? By faith.

Having faith and believing are often used interchangeably in God's Word. I don't think we have to wait for a special feel-ing in order to believe. It is something we decide to do based on God's faithfulness. God can be trusted—He does not lie, and He always does what He says He will do. Therefore, we can put our trust, faith, and belief in Him. The Amplified Bible, Classic Edi-tion describes faith as the assurance—the confirmation or title deed—of what we hope for:

> Now faith is the assurance (the confirmation, the title deed) of the things [we] hope for, being the proof of things [we] do not see and the conviction of their reality [faith perceiving as real fact what is not revealed to the senses].
>
> Hebrews 11:1 AMPC

If I were visiting you and told you I had a house and you asked to see my house, I couldn't show it to you right at that moment. But I could show you the *title deed* to the house, and then you would believe I had it. Faith is like that. We don't always see the result of it immediately, but we have the title deed in our heart because we believe the Word of God.

> *Faith is of the utmost importance because it is the way we receive from God.*

Faith is of the utmost importance because it is the way we receive from God. Without faith, we cannot please God (Hebrews 11:6). The just and righteous person lives by faith (Romans 1:17). No matter how many wonderful blessings God makes available to us, they do us no good unless we believe they are ours. A man could have a car in his garage with the keys in it, but if he didn't believe it was his, he could spend his life walking everywhere instead of driving.

This book focuses on being authentically and uniquely you, and doing that requires believing. We need to believe that we can be ourselves and still be accepted. Not everyone will accept us, but it is better to have fewer friends and be your unique self than to have many friends and feel you must alter yourself to do what they demand in order to be accepted. I mentioned earlier that when I took the step of faith to teach God's Word, I lost a lot of friends. It took faith for me to hold my ground in God and let go of people who were not true friends to me. I was lonely for a while, but when we obey God, He always rewards us in due time. Now I have more friends than I can keep up with.

Being who God has created you to be will require you to believe. Believe that it is better to be authentic than to be phony. Believe that God will open the right doors of opportunity for you at the right time. Believe that you have abilities beyond what you have experienced so far, and if you commit to authenticity, you will see them blossom. Believing the promises of God releases joy in your life. Simply put, if you believe God's promises, you will be happy. I am not suggesting that you can have anything you decide to believe you will have. But you can have anything God has promised you in His Word.

I am not a morning person, and it often takes me a while to get going. I am usually groggy and not very talkative first thing in the morning. I could easily dread each day if I based my anticipation of it on how I feel during the first fifteen minutes I am up. But instead of going by how I feel or what I may be inclined to think, I make a choice to believe God's Word and think, *"This is the day the Lord has made; [I] will rejoice and be glad in it"* (Psalm 118:24 NKJV). Then I remind myself that God has a good plan for me and that I can choose to believe that something good will happen to me and through me that day. I know that what I believe about the day ahead of me will greatly influence how it turns out, so I believe for the best.

## Beware of Dread

Just as God tells us not to fear, He also tells us not to dread. To dread means "to anticipate with fear or apprehension," and dread drains our zeal to do something before we even try to do it. Dread is fear in disguise. We often do not recognize it for the problem it is. We look ahead to things we know we need to do, and instead of believing they can be enjoyable, we believe they will be hard and unpleasant. For example, if I am going to the gym to work out in a couple of hours and then walk for one mile, I certainly could dread it if I didn't resist the temptation to do so. I have learned the uselessness and negativity of dreading activities I plan to do anyway, so I refuse to dread them. The choice is mine. The choice to dread or not to dread is also yours.

You can dread going to work, cleaning house, paying your bills, shopping at the grocery store, helping your child with a science project, or countless other responsibilities, but it will waste your energy. You have another much happier choice, which is to believe that God will help you do

> Enjoy everything you do and stay positive at all times by believing God's Word.

what you need to do when the time comes to do it. One of the best ways to defeat the devil is to enjoy everything you do and stay positive at all times by believing God's Word.

Defeat dread by not giving in to it. Dare to believe, and you too will see the glory of God manifested in your life.

> Do not let your hearts be troubled. You believe in God; believe also in me.
>
> John 14:1

This verse offers such a simple solution to our problems. We don't have to waste time and energy worrying, dreading, or being in fear. We can simply believe in God, in Jesus, and in the Holy Spirit. We can believe God's promises and His Word. We can live in the world and yet not be conformed to the world, but be transformed by the entire renewal of our minds (Romans 12:2). We can learn how to think as God thinks, and as we do, we will have the life Jesus died to give us.

## Living with Joy

Though you have not seen him, you love him; and even though you do not see him now, you believe in him and are filled with an inexpressible and glorious joy.

1 Peter 1:8

I want to leave you with the hope of having joy and enjoying your life, enjoying your unique self, and enjoying God. The scripture above shows us that the pathway to such a life is believing. Each of us can choose the kind of life we want to have. I urge you to choose well.

# CONCLUSION

Each time I finish a book, I feel as though I have given birth to a baby. In this book, I feel satisfied that I have given you the biblical information to live life authentically, with freedom to express your uniqueness. You have much to give to the world, and now is the time to begin doing it. It is a new day, a new beginning for anyone who needs or wants one.

Live to please God, not people. Love people, but don't let them control you. Be courageous enough to say no to requests from people when you don't believe you are supposed to do what they ask of you. Live with confidence, be bold, and don't fear rejection. It is for freedom that Jesus has set us free (Galatians 5:1), and He wants you to be free to be your amazing self.

Every life is a journey, and no matter where you are on your unique journey, you can make decisions that will enhance the remainder of it. *We all have a story that is unique, and it isn't finished yet.*

We all have a story that is unique, and it isn't finished yet. There are chapters of your personal story yet to come. Someday our story will say "The End," and when it does, we want to be satisfied that we have lived the best life we could have lived. We want to have no regrets, and we want to leave a legacy that will continue to benefit others for years to come.

Writing this book is part of my story and legacy, and I hope it adds freedom and joy to your journey.

Deuteronomy 7:9

1 Chronicles 16:34

2 Chronicles 6:14

Nehemiah 9:16–17

Psalm 17:7

Psalm 23

Psalm 25:6

Psalm 36:5–7

Psalm 63:3

Psalm 86:5

Psalm 86:15

Psalm 89:2

Psalm 103:8

Psalm 107:8–9

Psalm 109:21

Psalm 109:26

Psalm 119:64

Psalm 138:2

Psalm 143:12

Isaiah 40:11

Isaiah 41:10

Isaiah 43:4

Isaiah 49:16

Isaiah 54:10

Jeremiah 29:11

Jeremiah 31:3

Lamentations 3:22–23

Zephaniah 3:17

John 3:16

John 15:9

John 15:13

Romans 3:3–4

Romans 5:6

Romans 5:8–9

Romans 8:31–32

Romans 8:35–39

2 Corinthians 5:17–19

Galatians 2:20

Ephesians 2:4–5

Ephesians 2:8

Ephesians 3:17–19

2 Thessalonians 2:16

2 Thessalonians 3:5

1 Timothy 1:14

Titus 3:4–5

1 Peter 5:7

1 John 3:1

1 John 3:16

1 John 4:9–10

1 John 4:16

| | |
|---|---|
| Leviticus 19:18 | Galatians 5:22–23 |
| Proverbs 3:3–4 | Galatians 6:9–10 |
| Proverbs 10:12 | Ephesians 4:1–3 |
| Proverbs 15:1 | Ephesians 4:31–32 |
| Proverbs 17:17 | Ephesians 5:2 |
| Zechariah 7:8 | Philippians 2:3 |
| Matthew 5:7 | Colossians 3:8–10 |
| Matthew 5:43–48 | Colossians 3:12–14 |
| Matthew 7:3–5 | Colossians 4:5–6 |
| Matthew 18:15 | 1 Thessalonians 3:12 |
| Matthew 22:37–39 | 1 Thessalonians 5:11 |
| Mark 12:31 | Titus 3:1 |
| Luke 6:27–31 | Hebrews 12:14 |
| Luke 6:35 | Hebrews 13:2 |
| Luke 17:3–4 | James 1:19 |
| John 13:34–35 | James 2:8–9 |
| Romans 12:9–10 | 1 Peter 1:22 |
| Romans 12:13 | 1 Peter 2:17 |
| Romans 12:17–21 | 1 Peter 3:8 |
| Romans 13:8–10 | 1 Peter 4:8 |
| 1 Corinthians 1:10 | 1 John 2:10 |
| 1 Corinthians 13:4–7 | 1 John 3:14 |
| 1 Corinthians 16:14 | 1 John 3:18 |
| 2 Corinthians 13:11 | 1 John 4:7–12 |
| Galatians 5:13–14 | 1 John 4:21 |

## Do you have a real relationship with Jesus?

God loves you! He created you to be a special, unique, one-of-a-kind individual, and He has a specific purpose and plan for your life. And through a personal relationship with your Creator—God—you can discover a way of life that will truly satisfy your soul.

No matter who you are, what you've done, or where you are in your life right now, God's love and grace are greater than your sin—your mistakes. Jesus willingly gave His life so you can receive forgiveness from God and have new life in Him. He's just waiting for you to invite Him to be your Savior and Lord.

If you are ready to commit your life to Jesus and follow Him, all you have to do is ask Him to forgive your sins and give you a fresh start in the life you are meant to live. Begin by praying this prayer...

> *Lord Jesus, thank You for giving Your life for me and forgiving me of my sins so I can have a personal relationship with You. I am sincerely sorry for the mistakes I've made, and I know I need You to help me live right.*
>
> *Your Word says in Romans 10:9, "If you declare with your mouth, 'Jesus is Lord,' and believe in your heart that God raised him from the dead, you will be saved" (NIV). I believe You are the Son of God and confess You as my Savior and Lord. Take me just as I am, and work in my heart, making me the person You want me to be. I want to live for You, Jesus, and I am so grateful that You are giving me a fresh start in my new life with You today.*
>
> *I love You, Jesus!*

It's so amazing to know that God loves us so much! He wants to have a deep, intimate relationship with us that grows every day as we spend time with Him in prayer and Bible study. And we want to encourage you in your new life in Christ.

Please visit joycemeyer.org/salvation to request Joyce's book *A New Way of Living*, which is our gift to you. We also have other free resources online to help you make progress in pursuing everything God has for you.

Congratulations on your fresh start in your life in Christ! We hope to hear from you soon.

Joyce Meyer is one of the world's leading practical Bible teachers. A *New York Times* bestselling author, Joyce's books have helped millions of people find hope and restoration through Jesus Christ. Joyce's programs, *Enjoying Everyday Life* and *Everyday Answers with Joyce Meyer*, air around the world on television, radio, and the Internet. Through Joyce Meyer Ministries, Joyce teaches internationally on a number of topics with a particular focus on how the Word of God applies to our everyday lives. Her candid communication style allows her to share openly and practically about her experiences so others can apply what she has learned to their lives.

Joyce has authored more than one hundred books, which have been translated into more than one hundred languages, and over 65 million of her books have been distributed worldwide. Bestsellers include *Power Thoughts*; *The Confident Woman*; *Look Great, Feel Great*; *Starting Your Day Right*; *Ending Your Day Right*; *Approval Addiction*; *How to Hear from God*; *Beauty for Ashes*; and *Battlefield of the Mind*.

Joyce's passion to help hurting people is foundational to the vision of Hand of Hope, the missions arm of Joyce Meyer Ministries. Hand of Hope provides worldwide humanitarian outreaches such as feeding programs, medical care, orphanages, disaster response, human trafficking intervention and rehabilitation, and much more—always sharing the love and gospel of Christ.

JOYCE MEYER MINISTRIES

U.S. & FOREIGN OFFICE
ADDRESSES

**Joyce Meyer Ministries**
P.O. Box 655
Fenton, MO 63026
USA
(636) 349-0303

**Joyce Meyer Ministries—Canada**
P.O. Box 7700
Vancouver, BC V6B 4E2
Canada
(800) 868-1002

**Joyce Meyer Ministries—Australia**
Locked Bag 77
Mansfield Delivery Centre
Queensland 4122
Australia
(07) 3349 1200

**Joyce Meyer Ministries—England**
P.O. Box 1549
Windsor SL4 1GT
United Kingdom
01753 831102

**Joyce Meyer Ministries—South Africa**
P.O. Box 5
Cape Town 8000
South Africa
(27) 21-701-1056

**Joyce Meyer Ministries—Francophonie**
29 avenue Maurice Chevalier
77330 Ozoir la Ferriere
France

**Joyce Meyer Ministries—Germany**
Postfach 761001
22060 Hamburg
Germany
+49 (0)40 / 88 88 4 11 11

**Joyce Meyer Ministries—Netherlands**
Lorenzlaan 14
7002 HB Doetinchem
+31 657 555 9789

**Joyce Meyer Ministries—Russia**
P.O. Box 789
Moscow 101000
Russia
+7 (495) 727-14-68

*100 Inspirational Quotes*
*100 Ways to Simplify Your Life*
*21 Ways to Finding Peace and Happiness*
*Any Minute*
*Approval Addiction*
*The Approval Fix*
*The Battle Belongs to the Lord*
*Battlefield of the Mind**
*Battlefield of the Mind Bible*
*Battlefield of the Mind for Kids*
*Battlefield of the Mind for Teens*
*Battlefield of the Mind Devotional*
*Battlefield of the Mind New Testament*
*Be Anxious for Nothing**
*Being the Person God Made You to Be*
*Beauty for Ashes*
*Change Your Words, Change Your Life*
*Colossians: A Biblical Study*
*The Confident Mom*
*The Confident Woman*
*The Confident Woman Devotional*
*Do It Afraid**
*Do Yourself a Favor . . . Forgive*
*Eat the Cookie . . . Buy the Shoes*
*Eight Ways to Keep the Devil under Your Feet*
*Ending Your Day Right*
*Enjoying Where You Are on the Way to Where You Are Going*
*Ephesians: A Biblical Study*
*The Everyday Life Bible*
*The Everyday Life Psalms and Proverbs*
*Filled with the Spirit*
*Galatians: A Biblical Study*
*Good Health, Good Life*
*Habits of a Godly Woman*
*Healing the Soul of a Woman**
*Healing the Soul of a Woman Devotional*
*Hearing from God Each Morning*
*How to Age without Getting Old*
*How to Hear from God**
*How to Succeed at Being Yourself*
*I Dare You*
*If Not for the Grace of God**
*In Pursuit of Peace*
*In Search of Wisdom*